Growing in the Gospel

The Psalms Project Volume Seven

Discovering the Spiritual World through the Psalms – Psalm 61-70

Rev. Dr. Michael Harvey Koplitz

TABLE OF CONTENTS

The goal of this project:

This research project will examine the 150 psalms for the spiritual awareness each Psalm offers. Each Psalm will be examined by its language and the commentary of the Sages. The spiritual awareness analysis will be done in alignment with Ari's definition of the Tree of life, the Book of Creation, and the Zohar. Each verse of the Psalm will be rewritten using the intent of the language and spiritual commentary to convey its spiritual lesson.

The main resources:

The Zohar

The Book of Creation

Ari's writing on the Tree of Life and the Ten Sefirot

The Theological Wordbook of the Old Testament

Samson Hirsch's commentary on the Psalms

Tehillim – Psalms – A new translation with a commentary anthologized from the Talmudic and rabbinic sources

Accordance Bible Software

Psalm 61

New American Standard 1995	Hebrew

New American Standard 1995

Psa. 61:0 For the choir director; on a stringed instrument. *A Psalm* of David.

Psa. 61:1 [a]Hear my cry, O God;
[b]Give heed to my prayer.
2 From the [a]end of the earth I call to You when my heart is [b]faint;
Lead me to [c]the rock that is higher than I.
3 For You have been a [a]refuge for me,
A [b]tower of strength [1]against the enemy.
4 Let me [1a]dwell in Your tent forever;
Let me [b]take refuge in the shelter of Your wings. [2]Selah.

Psa. 61:5 For You have heard my [a]vows, O God;
You have given *me* the inheritance of those who [b]fear Your name.
6 You will [1a]prolong the king's [2]life;
His years will be as many generations.
7 He will [1]abide [a]before God forever;
Appoint [b]lovingkindness and truth that they may preserve him.

Hebrew

Psa. 61:1 לַמְנַצֵּחַ ׀ עַל־נְגִינַת
לְדָוִד ׃ ² שִׁמְעָה אֱלֹהִים
³ רִנָּתִי הַקְשִׁיבָה תְּפִלָּתִי ׃
מִקְצֵה הָאָרֶץ ׀ אֵלֶיךָ אֶקְרָא
בַּעֲטֹף לִבִּי בְּצוּר־יָרוּם
⁴ מִמֶּנִּי תַנְחֵנִי ׃ כִּי־הָיִיתָ
מַחְסֶה לִי מִגְדַּל־עֹז מִפְּנֵי
⁵ אוֹיֵב ׃ אָגוּרָה בְאָהָלְךָ
עוֹלָמִים אֶחֱסֶה בְסֵתֶר
⁶ כְנָפֶיךָ סֶּלָה ׃ כִּי־אַתָּה
אֱלֹהִים שָׁמַעְתָּ לִנְדָרָי נָתַתָּ
⁷ יְרֻשַּׁת יִרְאֵי שְׁמֶךָ ׃ יָמִים
עַל־יְמֵי־מֶלֶךְ תּוֹסִיף שְׁנוֹתָיו
⁸ כְּמוֹ־דֹר וָדֹר ׃ יֵשֵׁב עוֹלָם
לִפְנֵי אֱלֹהִים חֶסֶד וֶאֱמֶת מַן
⁹ יִנְצְרֻהוּ ׃ כֵּן אֲזַמְּרָה שִׁמְךָ
לָעַד לְשַׁלְּמִי נְדָרַי יוֹם ׀
יוֹם ׃

8 So I will *sing praise to Your name forever, That I may ᵇpay my vows day by day.	

References

Psalm 61:1
[a]Ps 64:1
[b]Ps 86:6

Psalm 61:2
[a]Ps 42:6
[b]Ps 77:3
[c]Ps 18:2; 94:22

Psalm 61:3
[1]Lit *from*
[a]Ps 62:7
[b]Ps 59:9; Prov 18:10

Psalm 61:4
[1]Or *sojourn*
[2]*Selah* may mean: *Pause, Crescendo* or *Musical interlude*
[a]Ps 23:6; 27:4
[b]Ps 17:8; 91:4

Psalm 61:5
[a]Job 22:27; Ps 56:12
[b]Deut 28:58; Neh 1:11; Ps 86:11; 102:15; Is 59:19; Mal 2:5; 4:2

Psalm 61:6
[1]Lit *add days to*
[2]Lit *days*
[a]Ps 21:4

Psalm 61:7
[1]Or *sit enthroned*
[a]Ps 41:12
[b]Ps 40:11

Psalm 61:8
[a]Judg 5:3; Ps 30:4; 33:2; 71:22
[b]Ps 65:1; Is 19:21

Targum

Psa. 61:1 For praise, with the psalms of David. [2] Accept, O LORD, my petition, hear my prayer. [3] From the ends of the earth I will pray in your presence when my heart is weary; lead me to a strong fortress built on a rock that is higher than I. [4] For you have been security for me, in truth, a stronghold before the enemy. [5] I will dwell in your tent forever, I will be secure in the shade of your presence forever. [6] For you, O LORD, have heard my vows; you have given the inheritance to those who fear your name. [7] You will add days to the age to come, the days of the King Messiah; his years are like the generations of this age and the generations of the age to come. [8] He will dwell forever in the presence of the LORD; goodness and truth from the Lord of the World will guard him. [9] Therefore, will I praise your name forever, when I pay my vows in the day of the redemption of Israel, and in the day the King Messiah is anointed to be king.

Spiritual Awareness

The spiritual rewrite for the verses is in bold.

Introduction

This Psalm demonstrates that no distance or danger could diminish David's fervent love for the LORD.

Verse one

נְגִינֹת (n'geenat) – means "instruments." In the context of this verse, this word denotes tones of a song inspired by and suited for all the various situations of physical and spiritual life.

David is speaking of the impact of his musical gifts, which exceeded his accomplishments as a warrior.

To the Sefirah Netzach who offers victory, upon the tones of song, a Psalm of David.

Verse two

Hear, O God, the outpouring of my spirit; attend to my prayer.

Verse three

The mind controls the body, which is visible to the outside world. If the spirit is weak, it will withdraw and hide behind the physical body. Therefore, a person needs a strong body and spirit.

If I call upon You from the end of the land when my heart shrouds itself, You will lead me to a rock that would be too high for me to ascend alone.

Verses four and five

In moments of anguish and weakness, it is good to know that one can rely on the LORD to be there.

For You have become a refuge for me, a tower of fortitude in the face of the enemy.

So I shall endeavor to dwell in Your tent forever, even when I shall rest hidden beneath the shade of your wings, as I trustingly hope to do. Meditate on this verse.

Verse six

David believed that his spiritual activities were his life's pledge and that the LORD accepted it with favor.

For you, O God, have heard my vows: You have granted them the heritage of those that fear Your Name.

Verse seven

David believed that the LORD gave him a longer life because of his spiritual activities. There is a midrash that says that Adam was shown David's rule and Adam decided to give David 25 years of his life.

You will add to my days as king; You will let his years be as the succession of generations.

Verse eight

David calls for the love and truth of the Sefirah Chesed for the time that he is on the throne of Israel.

But if he is to dwell before God forever, have the Sefirah Chesed place mercy and truth upon me.

Verse nine

Thus I will sing praises unto Your Name throughout all time, in order to perform my vows day by day.

Complete Psalm Rewrite Emphasizing Spiritual Awareness

To the Sefirah Netzach who offers victory, upon the tones of song, a Psalm of David. Hear, O God, the outpouring of my spirit; attend to my prayer.

If I call upon You from the end of the land when my heart shrouds itself, You will lead me to a rock that would be too high for me to ascend alone.

For You have become a refuge for me, a tower of fortitude in the face of the enemy.

So I shall endeavor to dwell in Your tent forever, even when I shall rest hidden beneath the shade of your wings, as I trustingly hope to do. Meditate on this verse.

For you, O God, have heard my vows: You have granted them the heritage of those that fear Your Name.

You will add to my days as king; You will let his years be as the succession of generations.

But if he is to dwell before God forever, have the Sefirah Chesed place mercy and truth upon me.

Thus I will sing praises unto Your Name throughout all time, in order to perform my vows day by day.

Psalm 62

New American Standard 1995	Hebrew

Psa. 62:0   For the choir director; †according to Jeduthun. A Psalm of David.

Psa. 62:1   *a*My soul *waits* in silence for God only;
From Him *b*is my salvation.
2   He only is my *a*rock and my salvation,
My *b*stronghold; I shall not be greatly shaken.

Psa. 62:3   How long will you assail a man,
That you may murder *him,* all of you,
Like a *a*leaning wall, like a tottering fence?
4   They have counseled only to thrust him down from his high position;
They *a*delight in falsehood;
They *b*bless with ¹their mouth,
But inwardly they curse.   ²Selah.

Psa. 62:5   My soul, *a*wait in silence for God only,
For my hope is from Him.
6   He only is *a*my rock and my salvation,
My stronghold; I shall not be shaken.
7   On God my *a*salvation and my glory *rest;*

אַ֫ל־יְד֫וּת֥וּן **Psa. 62:1** לַמְנַצֵּ֥חַ עַֽל־

מִזְמ֥וֹר לְדָוִֽד ׃ ² אַ֤ךְ אֶל־

אֱלֹהִ֭ים דּֽוּמִיָּ֣ה נַפְשִׁ֑י מִ֝מֶּ֗נּוּ

יְשׁוּעָתִֽי ׃ ³ אַךְ־ה֣וּא צ֭וּרִי

וִ֭ישׁוּעָתִ֑י מִ֝שְׂגַּבִּ֗י לֹא־אֶמּ֥וֹט

רַבָּֽה ׃ ⁴ עַד־אָ֤נָה ׀ תְּהֽוֹתְת֣וּ עַל

אִישׁ֮ תְּרָצְּח֪וּ כֻ֫לְּכֶ֥ם כְּקִ֥יר נָט֑וּי

גָּ֝דֵ֗ר הַדְּחוּיָֽה ׃ ⁵ אַ֤ךְ מִשְּׂאֵת֨וֹ ׀

יָעֲצ֣וּ לְהַדִּיחַ֮ יִרְצ֪וּ כָ֫זָ֥ב בְּפִ֥יו

יְבָרֵ֑כוּ וּֽבְקִרְבָּ֗ם יְקַלְלוּ־סֶֽלָה ׃ ⁶

אַ֤ךְ לֵֽאלֹהִ֗ים דּ֭וֹמִּי נַפְשִׁ֑י כִּי־

מִ֝מֶּ֗נּוּ תִּקְוָתִֽי ׃ ⁷ אַךְ־ה֣וּא צ֭וּרִי

וִישׁוּעָתִ֑י מִ֝שְׂגַּבִּ֗י לֹ֣א אֶמּֽוֹט ׃ ⁸

עַל־אֱ֭לֹהִים יִשְׁעִ֣י וּכְבוֹדִ֑י צוּר־

עֻזִּ֥י מַ֝חְסִ֗י בֵּֽאלֹהִֽים ׃ ⁹ בִּטְח֘וּ ב֤וֹ

בְכָל־עֵ֨ת ׀ עָ֗ם שִׁפְכֽוּ־לְפָנָ֥יו

לְבַבְכֶ֑ם אֱלֹהִ֖ים מַחֲסֶה־לָּ֣נוּ

סֶֽלָה ׃ ¹⁰ אַ֤ךְ ׀ הֶ֥בֶל בְּנֵֽי־אָדָ֡ם

כָּזָ֤ב בְּנֵ֫י אִ֥ישׁ בְּמֹאזְנַ֥יִם לַעֲל֑וֹת

הֵ֝֗מָּה מֵהֶ֥בֶל יָֽחַד ׃ ¹¹ אַל־

תִּבְטְח֬וּ בְעֹ֗שֶׁק וּבְגָזֵ֥ל אַל־

The rock of my strength, my [b]refuge is in God.

8 [a]Trust in Him at all times, O people;

[b]Pour out your heart before Him;

God is a refuge for us. Selah.

Psa. 62:9 Men of [a]low degree are only [b]vanity and men of rank are a [c]lie;

In the [d]balances they go up;

They are together lighter than breath.

10 [a]Do not trust in oppression

And do not [1]vainly hope in [b]robbery;

If riches increase, [c]do not set *your* heart *upon them.*

Psa. 62:11 [1]Once God has [a]spoken;

[2]Twice I have heard this:

That [b]power belongs to God;

12 And lovingkindness [a]is Yours, O Lord,

For You [b]recompense a man according to his work.

תֶּהְבָּלוּ חָיִל ׀ כִּי־יָנוּב אַל־
תָּשִׁיתוּ לֵב׃ אַחַת ׀ דִּבֶּר 12
אֱלֹהִים שְׁתַּיִם־זוּ שָׁמָעְתִּי כִּי עֹז
לֵאלֹהִים׃ וּלְךָ־אֲדֹנָי חָסֶד 13
כִּי־אַתָּה תְשַׁלֵּם לְאִישׁ
כְּמַעֲשֵׂהוּ׃

References

Psalm 62:0
[†]Cf 1 Chr 16:41; 25:1; Ps 39 and titles

Psalm 62:1
[a]Ps 33:20
[b]Ps 37:39

Psalm 62:2
[a]Ps 89:26
[b]Ps 59:17; 62:6

Psalm 62:3
[a]Is 30:13

Psalm 62:4
[1]Lit *his*
[2]*Selah* may mean: *Pause, Crescendo* or *Musical interlude*
[a]Ps 4:2
[b]Ps 28:3; 55:21

Psalm 62:5
[a]Ps 62:1

Psalm 62:6
[a]Ps 62:2

Psalm 62:7
[a]Ps 85:9; Jer 3:23
[b]Ps 46:1

Psalm 62:8
[a]Ps 37:3, 5; 52:8; Is 26:4
[b]1 Sam 1:15; Ps 42:4; Lam 2:19

Psalm 62:9
[a]Ps 49:2
[b]Job 7:16; Ps 39:5; Is 40:17
[c]Ps 116:11

[d]Is 40:15

Psalm 62:10

[1]Lit *become vain in robbery*
[a]Is 30:12
[b]Is 61:8; Ezek 22:29; Nah 3:1
[c]Job 31:25; Ps 49:6; 52:7; Mark 10:24; Luke 12:15; 1 Tim 6:10

Psalm 62:11

[1]Or *One thing*
[2]Or *These two things I have heard*
[a]Job 33:14; 40:5
[b]Ps 59:17; Rev 19:1

Psalm 62:12

[a]Ps 86:5; 103:8; 130:7
[b]Job 34:11; Ps 28:4; Jer 17:10; Matt 16:27; Rom 2:6; 1 Cor 3:8; Rev 2:23

Targum

Psa. 62:1 For praise, by Jeduthun. A psalm of David. **²** Truly, for God my soul is quiet; from him is my redemption. **³** Truly, he is my strength and my redemption, my savior, I shall not be shaken on the day of great distress. **⁴** How long do you rage against a pious man? All of you will be slain, like a crooked wall, like a broken fence. **⁵** Truly, when they swear to do good, they take counsel to attack; they will tell lies; with their mouth they will bless and with their heart they will curse forever. **⁶** Truly, be silent for God, O my soul, for my hope comes from him. **⁷** Truly, he is my strength and my redemption, my savior, I shall not be shaken. **⁸** My redemption and my honor is on God; the strength of my might, my hope, is in God. **⁹** Hope in his word at all times, O people of the house of Israel; pour out the pride of your hearts in his presence; say, "God is our hope forever." **¹⁰** For the sons of men are nothing, the sons of a man are deceit; when they take wives, their fates are weighed in the balances; they themselves came to be altogether out of nothing. **¹¹** Do not trust in oppression, and do not receive money gained by coercion; for [though] it will increase in value, do not set your mind [on it]. **¹²** God speaks one Torah, and now two times I have heard it, from the mouth of Moses, the great scribe, for there is might in the presence of God. **¹³** And it is yours, O God, to show favor to the righteous, for you repay each man according to his works.

Spiritual Awareness

Introduction

David was being pursued by his enemies, who were set on killing him. Even in the face of these enemies, David never lost hope or faith that the LORD would take care of him. The enemies were wealthy people who could buy murderers to kill David. David's faith demonstrates that it is best to have faith in the LORD and not in money or riches. The sage Rashi calls this Psalm the hymn of Israel during the Exile.

Superscript

According to Rabbi Hirsch יְדִיתוּן is not the name of a person. He compared the Hebrew word structure and noted that it is the same as Psalm 77. If this is a name, it is not easy to understand his relationship with David. This name can be found in 1 Chronicles 16:41-42. It is not clear from this passage if Jeduthun was the choir director. Therefore, Hirsch believes that Jeduthun is not a name.

יְדִיתוּן (ydeeton) root word means "hand" and, in its form, denotes the activity of the hand. It means the eternally constant Divine providence as demonstrated in the fate of individuals.

To the Sefirah Netzach who gives victory over an enemy, upon the providences of God's hand, a psalm of David.

Verse one

The basic theme of the Psalm is that even when the hand of the LORD strikes us with pain and sorrow, we can turn to none but Him for comfort. The LORD is always a source of help.

Only toward God does my soul wait in silence; my salvation comes from Him.

Verse two

He is my rock, my salvation, and my stronghold; I shall not be significantly swayed.

Verse three

This is a difficult verse to interpret. It contains several words that are only found in this Psalm in their grammatical format. Hirsch offers the following translation.

How long will you seek to strike terror into a man, as if all of you were threatened by murder as if the mere leaning of a wall, the fence has already been cast down?

Verse four

לְהַדִּיחַ – l'hadeecha, "to induce a person to deviate from the right path."

They have plotted only to lure him down from his lofty station; they have chosen deceit; they bless with his speech but curse within their hearts. Meditate on this verse.

Verses five & six

David firmly repeats that he will not stray from the LORD no matter what happens.

The LORD is the sole source of David's peace of mind for that day and every day. Only before God be silent, my soul, for my hope comes from him.

He alone is my Rock and my Salvation, my stronghold, and I shall certainly not be swayed.

Verse seven

In the light of danger and possible death, David calls out to the LORD for help. All of his hopes will always rest with the LORD.

With God is my salvation and my glory; the rock of my fortitude and my refuge is in God.

Verse eight

David envisioned himself in the "school of suffering." He wanted to tell all his people the conviction that he learned that the LORD is in charge even in suffering.

Trust in the LORD at all times, O people; pour out your hearts before Him; God is a refuge unto us. Meditate upon this passage.

Verse nine

The LORD is always with his people. He is unchangeable, regardless of whether He blesses us with joy or afflicts us with grief.

However, the sons of man are to no purpose, and the sons of men are deceitful; all of them together can be made to spring up by a breath upon the scales.

Verse ten

You cannot look toward humans for help because, most times you will not receive any. Therefore, put your trust in the LORD, who will protect you and your property.

Put not your trust in property unlawfully withheld nor make yourselves as naughty by robbery; even when your riches flourish in accord with right, set not your heart upon them.

Verses eleven & twelve

David learned two lessons. First is that the LORD is invincible in His might; second, the LORD is unchangeable.

One thing has God spoken; I have heard this dual truth therein; that steadfastness belongs to God.

And that to You, my Master, it is mercy when You reward every man in accordance with his acts.

Complete Psalm Rewrite Emphasizing Spiritual Awareness

To the Sefirah Netzach who gives victory over an enemy, upon the providences of God's hand, a psalm of David.

Only toward God does my soul wait in silence; my salvation comes from Him. He is my rock, my salvation, and my stronghold; I shall not be significantly swayed. How long will you seek to strike terror into a man, as if all of you were threatened by murder as if the mere leaning of a wall, the fence has already been cast down? They have plotted only to lure him down from his lofty station; they have chosen deceit; they bless with his speech but curse within their hearts. Meditate on this verse.

The LORD is the sole source of David's peace of mind for that day and every day. Only before God be silent, my soul, for my hope comes from him.

He alone is my Rock and my Salvation, my stronghold, and I shall certainly not be swayed.

With God is my salvation and my glory; the rock of my fortitude and my refuge is in God.

Trust in the LORD at all times, O people; pour out your hearts before Him; God is a refuge unto us. Meditate upon this passage.

However, the sons of man are to no purpose, and the sons of men are deceitful; all of them together can be made to spring up by a breath upon the scales.

Put not your trust in property unlawfully withheld nor make yourselves as naughty by robbery; even when your riches flourish in accord with right, set not your heart upon them.

One thing has God spoken; I have heard this dual truth therein; that steadfastness belongs to God.

And that to You, my Master, it is mercy when You reward every man in accordance with his acts.

Psalm 63

New American Standard 1995	Hebrew
Psa. 63:0 A Psalm of David, [†]when he was in the wilderness of Judah.	מִזְמוֹר לְדָוִד בִּהְיוֹתוֹ **Psa. 63:1**
Psa. 63:1 O God, [a]You are my God; I shall seek You [1]earnestly;	בְּמִדְבַּר יְהוּדָה׃ 2 אֱלֹהִים |
My soul [b]thirsts for You, my flesh [2]yearns for You,	אֵלִי אַתָּה אֲשַׁחֲרֶךָּ צָמְאָה לְךָ |
In a [c]dry and weary land where there is no water.	נַפְשִׁי כָּמַהּ לְךָ בְשָׂרִי בְּאֶרֶץ־
[2] Thus I have [a]seen You in the Sanctuary,	צִיָּה וְעָיֵף בְּלִי־מָיִם׃ 3 כֵּן
To see Your power and Your glory.	בַּקֹּדֶשׁ חֲזִיתִךָ לִרְאוֹת עֻזְּךָ
[3] Because Your [a]lovingkindness is better than life,	וּכְבוֹדֶךָ׃ 4 כִּי־טוֹב חַסְדְּךָ
My lips will praise You.	מֵחַיִּים שְׂפָתַי יְשַׁבְּחוּנְךָ׃ 5 כֵּן
[4] So I will bless You [a]as long as I live; I will [b]lift up my hands in Your name.	אֲבָרֶכְךָ בְחַיָּי בְּשִׁמְךָ אֶשָּׂא
[5] My soul is [a]satisfied as with [1]marrow and fatness,	כַפָּי׃ 6 כְּמוֹ חֵלֶב וָדֶשֶׁן תִּשְׂבַּע
And my mouth offers [b]praises with joyful lips.	נַפְשִׁי וְשִׂפְתֵי רְנָנוֹת יְהַלֶּל־פִּי׃ 7
Psa. 63:6 When I remember You [a]on my bed,	אִם־זְכַרְתִּיךָ עַל־יְצוּעָי
I meditate on You in the [b]night watches,	בְּאַשְׁמֻרוֹת אֶהְגֶּה־בָּךְ׃ 8 כִּי־
[7] For [a]You have been my help,	הָיִיתָ עֶזְרָתָה לִּי וּבְצֵל כְּנָפֶיךָ
And in the [b]shadow of Your wings I sing for joy.	אֲרַנֵּן׃ 9 דָּבְקָה נַפְשִׁי אַחֲרֶיךָ
[8] My soul [a]clings [1]to You; Your [b]right hand upholds me.	בִּי תָּמְכָה יְמִינֶךָ׃ 10 וְהֵמָּה
Psa. 63:9 But those who [a]seek my [1]life to destroy it,	לְשׁוֹאָה יְבַקְשׁוּ נַפְשִׁי יָבֹאוּ
	בְּתַחְתִּיּוֹת הָאָרֶץ׃ 11 יַגִּירֻהוּ
	עַל־יְדֵי־חָרֶב מְנָת שֻׁעָלִים
	יִהְיוּ׃ 12 וְהַמֶּלֶךְ יִשְׂמַח בֵּאלֹהִים
	יִתְהַלֵּל כָּל־הַנִּשְׁבָּע בּוֹ כִּי
	יִסָּכֵר פִּי דוֹבְרֵי־שָׁקֶר׃

Will go into the [2b]depths of the earth.

10   [1]They will be [2a]delivered over to the power of the sword;

They will be a [3b]prey for foxes.

11   But the [a]king will rejoice in God;

Everyone who [b]swears by Him will glory,

For the [c]mouths of those who speak lies will be stopped.

References

Psalm 63:0
'1 Sam 22:5; 23:14

Psalm 63:1
[1]Lit *early*
[2]Lit *faints*
[a]Ps 118:28
[b]Ps 42:2; 84:2; Matt 5:6
[c]Ps 143:6

Psalm 63:2
[a]Ps 27:4

Psalm 63:3
[a]Ps 69:16

Psalm 63:4
[a]Ps 104:33; 146:2
[b]Ps 28:2; 143:6

Psalm 63:5
[1]Lit *fat*
[a]Ps 36:8
[b]Ps 71:23

Psalm 63:6
[a]Ps 4:4
[b]Ps 16:7; 42:8; 119:55

Psalm 63:7
[a]Ps 27:9
[b]Ps 17:8

Psalm 63:8
[1]Lit *after*
[a]Num 32:12; Deut 1:36; Hos 6:3
[b]Ps 18:35; 41:12

Psalm 63:9
[1]Lit *soul*
[2]Lit *lowest places*
[a]Ps 40:14
[b]Ps 55:15

Psalm 63:10
[1]Lit *They will pour him out*
[2]Lit *poured out by*
[3]Lit *portion*
[a]Jer 18:21; Ezek 35:5
[b]Lam 5:18

Psalm 63:11
[a]Ps 21:1
[b]Deut 6:13; Is 45:23; 65:16
[c]Job 5:16; Ps 107:42; Rom 3:19

Targum

Psa. 63:1 A psalm of David, when he was in the wilderness in the territory of the tribe of Judah. [2] O God, you are my strength; I will arise in the morning in your presence; my soul thirsts for you, my flesh yearns for you, in a barren and weary land, without water. [3] Thus I have seen you in the holy place; purify me to see your strength and your glory. [4] For better is the favor that you show to the righteous in the age to come than the life you have given to the wicked in this age; therefore my lips will praise you. [5] Thus will I bless you in my life in this age; in the name of your word I will spread my hands in prayer in the age to come. [6] My soul will be satisfied as with fat and oil, and my mouth shall sing [with] lips of praise. [7] If I have remembered you on my bed, in the night-watch I will meditate on your word. [8] For you were a helper to me, and in the shade of your presence I will be glad. [9] My soul has followed close behind your Torah; your right hand has supported me. [10] But they will seek my soul for the grave; they will enter the lowest part of the earth. [11] They will fear him on account of the blow of the sword; they will be the portion of jackals. [12] And the king will rejoice in the word of God; all who swear by his word will sing praise, for the mouth of those who speak deceit will be stifled.

Spiritual Awareness

Introduction

David discloses his spiritual thirst while in the wilderness, pursued by Saul's men trying to kill him. He built a fortress of faith that shielded him from what was happening outside his hiding place.

Verse one

David came to realize that the LORD is not impersonal. The LORD wants a relationship with all the souls on the earth.

O God, You are my God; at early dawn will I seek You. My soul thirsts for You, my flesh longs for You in the barren land, and it grows faith without water.

Verses two & three

David developed a kind of spiritual perception of the heart rather than that of the eye. The LORD cannot be seen. However, the presence of the LORD through the Shekinah can be sensed. During David's isolation, his spirit could feel the presence of the LORD with him.

Thus I have perceived You in the Sanctuary to see Your invincible power and glory.

The mercy and love from the Sefirah Chesed are better than life; thus, my lips were wont to praise you.

Verse four

בְּשִׁמְךָ אֶשָּׂא כַפָּי (b'sheem'cha asa kafa) – "lift up my hands in your Name." This phrase references the palm of the hand that is bent and about to close to grasp an object. A hand in this position, but empty, raised to God, symbolizes a plea to Him to supply us with what we lack.

So will I also bless You now through my life; in Your Name shall I lift up my hands.

Verse five

When David connected with the LORD, his spiritual thirst was satisfied.

Then my soul shall be satisfied as with fat and marrow, and my mouth will praise Your mighty acts with joyous lips.

Verses six & seven

David said that he felt the LORD's presence through the Shekinah while on a couch, which was most likely in the palace. He could feel the LORD's presence while in the cave.

While [in days past] I remembered You upon my couch, I will now meditate upon You during night watches.

For You have been my help, and in the shadow of Your wings will I joyfully sing.

Verse eight

My soul cleaves after You; Your right hand has held me fast.

Verse nine

Saul's men chased David into the Judean wilderness, and they believed that they would capture and kill David.

But they seek my soul to destroy it; it shall go into the nethermost depths of the earth.

Verse ten

They who would have let it be spent by the sword shall be the prey of foxes.

Verse eleven

Even with Saul's men chasing him, David still paid homage to his king. He was sincere in his thoughts about King Saul.

But let the king rejoice in God, let anyone that swears by him glory; for the mouths of them that utter lies shall fall silent.

Complete Psalm Rewrite Emphasizing Spiritual Awareness

O God, You are my God; at early dawn will I seek You. My soul thirsts for You, my flesh longs for You in the barren land, and it grows faith without water.

Thus I have perceived You in the Sanctuary to see Your invincible power and glory.

The mercy and love from the Sefirah Chesed are better than life; thus, my lips were wont to praise you.

So will I also bless You now through my life; in Your Name shall I lift up my hands.

Then my soul shall be satisfied as with fat and marrow, and my mouth will praise Your mighty acts with joyous lips.
While [in days past] I remembered You upon my couch, I will now meditate upon You during night watches.

For You have been my help, and in the shadow of Your wings will I joyfully sing.

My soul cleaves after You; Your right hand has held me fast.
But they seek my soul to destroy it; it shall go into the nethermost depths of the earth.

They who would have let it be spent by the sword shall be the prey of foxes.

But let the king rejoice in God, let anyone that swears by him glory; for the mouths of them that utter lies shall fall silent.

Psalm 64

New American Standard 1995	Hebrew
Psa. 64:0 For the choir director. A Psalm of David.	לַמְנַצֵּחַ מִזְמֹור **Psa. 64:1**
Psa. 64:1 Hear my voice, O God, in [a]my [1]complaint;	לְדָוִד ׃ ² שְׁמַע־אֱלֹהִים קֹולִי
[b]Preserve my life from dread of the enemy.	בְשִׂיחִי מִפַּחַד אֹויֵב תִּצֹּר
2 Hide me from the [a]secret counsel of evildoers,	חַיָּי ׃ ³ תַּסְתִּירֵנִי מִסֹּוד
From the tumult of [b]those who do iniquity,	מְרֵעִים מֵרִגְשַׁת פֹּעֲלֵי אָוֶן ׃ ⁴
3 Who [a]have sharpened their tongue like a sword.	אֲשֶׁר שָׁנְנוּ כַחֶרֶב לְשֹׁונָם
They [b]aimed bitter speech *as* their arrow,	דָּרְכוּ חִצָּם דָּבָר מָר ׃ ⁵
4 To [a]shoot [1]from concealment at the blameless;	לִירֹות בַּמִּסְתָּרִים תָּם פִּתְאֹם
Suddenly they shoot at him, and [b]do not fear.	יֹרֻהוּ וְלֹא יִירָאוּ ׃ ⁶ יְחַזְּקוּ־
5 They [1]hold fast to themselves an evil purpose;	לָמֹו ׀ דָּבָר רָע יְסַפְּרוּ
They [2]talk of [a]laying snares secretly;	לִטְמֹון מֹוקְשִׁים אָמְרוּ מִי
They say, "[b]Who can see them?"	יִרְאֶה־לָּמֹו ׃ ⁷ יַחְפְּשׂוּ־עֹולֹת
6 They [1]devise injustices, *saying,*	תַּמְנוּ חֵפֶשׂ מְחֻפָּשׂ וְקֶרֶב
"We are [2]ready with a well-conceived plot";	אִישׁ וְלֵב עָמֹק ׃ ⁸ וַיֹּרֵם
For the [3a]inward thought and the heart of a man are [4]deep.	אֱלֹהִים חֵץ פִּתְאֹום הָיוּ
Psa. 64:7 But [a]God [1]will shoot at them with an arrow;	מַכֹּותָם ׃ ⁹ וַיַּכְשִׁילוּהוּ עָלֵימֹו
Suddenly [2]they will be wounded.	לְשֹׁונָם יִתְנֹדֲדוּ כָּל־רֹאֵה
8 So [1]they [2]will [a]make him stumble;	בָם ׃ ¹⁰ וַיִּירְאוּ כָּל־אָדָם
[b]Their own tongue is against them;	וַיַּגִּידוּ פֹּעַל אֱלֹהִים וּמַעֲשֵׂהוּ
	הִשְׂכִּילוּ ׃ ¹¹ יִשְׂמַח צַדִּיק

<table>
<tr><td>

All who see them will [c]shake the head.
9   Then all men [1]will [a]fear,
And they [2]will [b]declare the work of God,
And [3]will consider [4]what He has done.
10   The righteous man will be [a]glad in the LORD and will [b]take refuge in Him;
And all the upright in heart will glory.

</td><td>

בַּיהוָה וְחָסָה בּוֹ וְיִתְהַלְלוּ
כָּל־יִשְׁרֵי־לֵב׃

</td></tr>
</table>

References

Psalm 64:1
[1]Or *concern*
[a]Ps 55:2
[b]Ps 140:1

Psalm 64:2
[a]Ps 56:6
[b]Ps 59:2

Psalm 64:3
[a]Ps 140:3
[b]Ps 58:7

Psalm 64:4
[1]Lit *in*
[a]Ps 10:8; 11:2
[b]Ps 55:19

Psalm 64:5
[1]Lit *make firm*
[2]Lit *tell of*
[a]Ps 140:5
[b]Job 22:13; Ps 10:11

Psalm 64:6
[1]Or *search out*
[2]Lit *complete*
[3]Or *inward part*
[4]Or *unsearchable*
[a]Ps 49:11

Psalm 64:7
[1]Or *shot*
[2]Or *they were wounded;* lit *their wounds occurred*
[a]Ps 7:12, 13

Psalm 64:8
[1]Or *they make their tongue a stumbling for themselves*
[2]Or *made*
[a]Ps 9:3
[b]Prov 12:13; 18:7
[c]Ps 22:7; 44:14; Jer 18:16; 48:27; Lam 2:15

Psalm 64:9

[1]Or *feared*
[2]Or *declared*
[3]Or *considered*
[4]Lit *His work*
[a]Ps 40:3
[b]Jer 51:10

Psalm 64:10
[a]Job 22:19; Ps 32:11
[b]Ps 11:1; 25:20

Targum

Psa. 64:1 For praise, a psalm of David. [2] Hear my voice, O God, in the time of my prayer; guard my life from the fear of the enemy. [3] You will hide me from the secret [council] of those who do evil, from the turmoil of those who practice deceit. [4] Who have sharpened their tongue as a sword, bent their bows, smeared their arrows with deadly and bitter poison. [5] To shoot in secret, without blame; suddenly they will shoot him and they will not fear. [6] They will strengthen themselves with an evil word; they will talk of hiding traps, saying, "Who sees them?" [7] They will search to find pretexts to destroy the pure, a search carried out in the body of a son of man, and the thoughts of a secret heart. [8] But God will shoot arrows at them suddenly; and they will tell of their wounds. [9] And their tongue will make them stumble; all who see them shall move aside. [10] And all the sons of men will be afraid, and tell of the work of the LORD God; and his works will be understood. [11] The righteous man will rejoice in the LORD, and trust in his word, and all the upright of heart will boast.

Spiritual Awareness

Introduction

This Psalm portrays the impudence of the word slander in all its dangerous connotations. It also says that slanders will eventually perish.

Superscript

David calls out to the Sefirah Netzach for victory over his enemies.

To the Sefirah Netzach, who grants victory, a psalm of David.

Verse one

שְׁמַ֫ע (sh'ma) means "hear"; however, in this context, it denotes inner growth of the mind and spirit.

O God hear my need to grow in mind and spirit; preserve my life from the fear of my foes.

Verses two, three, and four

David felt that only the LORD could protect him from a plot against him which was made in secret. Secrecy was considered a deadly weapon.

You alone can hide me from the secret counsel of evildoers, from the tumult of the workers of violence.

Who have sharpened their tongues like a sword and have aimed the bitter word as their arrow.

In order to strike the blameless man in secret places. They wish to strike him unaware, and they are not afraid.

Verse five

David's slanderers believed that the evil words they spoke are a strong weapon.

They think the evil word is strong; they lay hidden snares as they tell; they say, who would see them?

Verse six

A physical act of evil is traceable and can be investigated. However, a spoken word act of evil at times goes beyond recall unless it is recorded verbatim.

Let them investigate the iniquities; we shall be here no more when a search is done, for the man is within, and the heart is deep.

Verse seven

David's enemies felt safe slandering him. However, the LORD smote them with His arrows.

Then God smote them. A sudden arrow, their blows came to be.

Verses eight, nine, and ten

And they made their own tongue a stumbling block unto themselves; all those who look upon them feel moved.

And all men learned to fear, and they declared it as the work of God and understood His acts.

Let him who is righteous rejoice in God and take refuge in Him, and let all the upright in heart glory.

Complete Psalm Rewrite Emphasizing Spiritual Awareness

O God hear my need to grow in mind and spirit; preserve my life from the fear of my foes.

You alone can hide me from the secret counsel of evildoers, from the tumult of the workers of violence.

Who have sharpened their tongues like a sword and have aimed the bitter word as their arrow.

In order to strike the blameless man in secret places. They wish to strike him unaware, and they are not afraid.

They think the evil word is strong; they lay hidden snares as they tell; they say, who would see them?

Let them investigate the iniquities; we shall be here no more when a search is done, for the man is within, and the heart is deep.

Let them investigate the iniquities; we shall be here no more when a search is done, for the man is within, and the heart is deep.

Then God smote them. A sudden arrow, their blows came to be.

Let him who is righteous rejoice in God and take refuge in Him, and let all the upright in heart glory.

Psalm 65

New American Standard 1995	Hebrew
Psa. 65:0 For the choir director. A Psalm of David. A Song. **Psa. 65:1** There will be silence [1]before You, *and* praise in Zion, O God, And to You the [a]vow will be performed. 2 O You who hear prayer, To You [a]all [1]men come. 3 [1][a]Iniquities prevail against me; As for our transgressions, You [2][b]forgive them. 4 How [a]blessed is the one whom You [b]choose and bring near *to You* To dwell in Your courts. We will be [c]satisfied with the goodness of Your house, Your holy temple. **Psa. 65:5** By [a]awesome *deeds* You answer us in righteousness, O [b]God of our salvation, You who are the trust of all the [c]ends of the earth and of the farthest [1][d]sea; 6 Who [a]establishes the mountains by His strength, Being [b]girded with might; 7 Who [a]stills the roaring of the seas, The roaring of their waves, And the [b]tumult of the peoples. 8 They who dwell in the [a]ends *of the earth* stand in awe of Your signs; You make the [1]dawn and the sunset shout for joy.	**Psa. 65:1** לַמְנַצֵּחַ מִזְמוֹר לְדָוִד 2 שִׁיר ׃ לְךָ דֻמִיָּה תְהִלָּה אֱלֹהִים בְּצִיּוֹן וּלְךָ יְשֻׁלַּם־ 3 נֶדֶר ׃ שֹׁמֵעַ תְּפִלָּה עָדֶיךָ כָּל־בָּשָׂר יָבֹאוּ ׃ 4 דִּבְרֵי עֲוֺנֹת גָּבְרוּ מֶנִּי פְּשָׁעֵינוּ אַתָּה תְכַפְּרֵם ׃ 5 אַשְׁרֵי ׀ תִּבְחַר וּתְקָרֵב יִשְׁכֹּן חֲצֵרֶיךָ נִשְׂבְּעָה בְּטוּב בֵּיתֶךָ קְדֹשׁ הֵיכָלֶךָ ׃ 6 נוֹרָאוֹת ׀ בְּצֶדֶק תַּעֲנֵנוּ אֱלֹהֵי יִשְׁעֵנוּ מִבְטָח כָּל־קַצְוֵי־אֶרֶץ וְיָם רְחֹקִים ׃ 7 מֵכִין הָרִים בְּכֹחוֹ נֶאְזָר בִּגְבוּרָה ׃ 8 מַשְׁבִּיחַ ׀ שְׁאוֹן יַמִּים שְׁאוֹן גַּלֵּיהֶם וַהֲמוֹן לְאֻמִּים ׃ 9 וַיִּירְאוּ ׀ וְיֹשְׁבֵי קְצָוֺת מֵאוֹתֹתֶיךָ מוֹצָאֵי־בֹקֶר וָעֶרֶב תַּרְנִין ׃ 10 פָּקַדְתָּ הָאָרֶץ ׀ וַתְּשֹׁקְקֶהָ רַבַּת תַּעְשְׁרֶנָּה פֶּלֶג אֱלֹהִים מָלֵא

Psa. 65:9 You visit the earth and [a]cause it to overflow;

You greatly [b]enrich it;

The [1][c]stream of God is full of water;

You prepare their [d]grain, for thus You prepare [2]the earth.

10 You water its furrows abundantly,

You [1]settle its ridges,

You soften it [a]with showers,

You bless its growth.

11 You have crowned the year [1]with Your [2][a]bounty,

And Your [3]paths [b]drip *with* fatness.

12 [a]The pastures of the wilderness drip,

And the [b]hills gird themselves with rejoicing.

13 The meadows are [a]clothed with flocks

And the valleys are [b]covered with grain;

They [c]shout for joy, yes, they sing.

מַיִם תָּכִין דְּגָנָם כִּי־כֵן
תְּכִינֶהָ : 11 תְּלָמֶיהָ רַוֵּה נַחֵת
גְּדוּדֶיהָ בִּרְבִיבִים תְּמֹגְגֶנָּה
צִמְחָהּ תְּבָרֵךְ : 12 עִטַּרְתָּ שְׁנַת
טוֹבָתֶךָ וּמַעְגָּלֶיךָ יִרְעֲפוּן
דָּשֶׁן : 13 יִרְעֲפוּ נְאוֹת מִדְבָּר
וְגִיל גְּבָעוֹת תַּחְגֹּרְנָה : 14
לָבְשׁוּ כָרִים הַצֹּאן וַעֲמָקִים
יַעַטְפוּ־בָר יִתְרוֹעֲעוּ אַף־
יָשִׁירוּ :

References

Psalm 64:1
[1]Or *concern*
[a]Ps 55:2
[b]Ps 140:1

Psalm 64:2
[a]Ps 56:6
[b]Ps 59:2

Psalm 64:3
[a]Ps 140:3
[b]Ps 58:7

Psalm 64:4
[1]Lit *in*
[a]Ps 10:8; 11:2
[b]Ps 55:19

Psalm 64:5
[1]Lit *make firm*
[2]Lit *tell of*
[a]Ps 140:5
[b]Job 22:13; Ps 10:11

Psalm 64:6
[1]Or *search out*
[2]Lit *complete*
[3]Or *inward part*
[4]Or *unsearchable*
[a]Ps 49:11

Psalm 64:7
[1]Or *shot*
[2]Or *they were wounded;* lit *their wounds occurred*
[a]Ps 7:12, 13

Psalm 64:8
[1]Or *they make their tongue a stumbling for themselves*

[2] Or *made*
[a] Ps 9:3
[b] Prov 12:13; 18:7
[c] Ps 22:7; 44:14; Jer 18:16; 48:27; Lam 2:15

Psalm 64:9

[1] Or *feared*
[2] Or *declared*
[3] Or *considered*
[4] Lit *His work*
[a] Ps 40:3
[b] Jer 51:10

Psalm 64:10

[a] Job 22:19; Ps 32:11
[b] Ps 11:1; 25:20

Targum

Psa. 65:1 For praise, a psalm of David, a song. [2] Before you praise is considered as silence, O God, whose presence is in Zion, and vows will be paid to you. [3] O receiver of prayer, unto you all the sons of flesh will come. [4] Words of iniquity have overcome me; you will atone for our sins. [5] How happy the one you will choose and bring near; he will abide in your courts. The righteous will say, "We will be satisfied in the goodness of your house, the holiness of your temple." [6] Accept our prayer [with] fearful deeds in righteousness, O God our redemption, the hope of all the ends of the earth, and the islands of the sea far from dry land. [7] Who established food for the ibexes of the mountains in the strength of his might, who is girded with a belt in might. [8] Who quiets the commotion of the seas and the commotion of their waves, and the hubbub of the nations. [9] And those who dwell at the borders were afraid at your signs; [at the] extremities of morning and evening you will set praise in their mouth. [10] You have remembered the land and watered it; you will enrich it with much produce from the vault of God which is in heaven, full of rain; you will form their grain, for thus you will consummate it. [11] He has drenched those raised on its plants; he has given rest to its troops; you will bless its blossoms. [12] You have crowned the year with the goodness of your blessings; and the paths of your way will give an odor of richness. [13] They will make sweet the psalms of the wilderness, and the hills will gird themselves with joy. [14] The rams will copulate with the flock, and the plains will be covered with grain; they will shout, indeed, they will rejoice.

Spiritual Awareness

Introduction

King David wrote this Psalm as a three-year famine had struck Israel. David prays for rain and an abundant crop. Droughts were devasting to the economy of Israel. She was an agriculturally based economy. More importantly, it meant that people were starving to death. David called upon the Sefirah Netzach, who offers spiritual victory.

To the Sefirah Netzach who grants spiritual victory, a Psalm, a Song of David.

Verse one

אֱלֹהִים בְּצִיּוֹן (ehlohim b'tzion), means "God of Zion." It is only in Zion that God made known to humanity that He was near and reveals his presence within the spirit of all. This is where the Neshamah of the soul can be most stirred.

Security and freedom from frustration, worry, and fear can be attained only by trusting the LORD and asking for His help.

Peace of soul is an emanation of Your mighty acts, O God in Zion, and unto you the vow is made.

Verse two

The peace of the soul is an inner activity of mind and spirit. This peace is perceived only by the LORD. Humans can create an intimate relationship with the LORD through the peace of the soul.

Of You Who hears prayer! One day all those that can feel will come unto You.

Verses three and four

Verse three contains an acknowledgment of the total evolution of human history. Individuals create complex situations brought about by their manifold errors that have grown too complex to fend off. The result is a disastrous situation.

The products of sin that are our common defection have overcome me; You will grant them atonement.

For only he whom You will choose and will bring near unto You strides forward to salvation, so that he may find a dwelling place in You courts. We too wish to be satisfied by the goodness of Your House, which is sanctified in the Abode of your might.

Verse five

The shaping of humankind's affairs is to follow righteousness taught us through the LORD's Torah.

You answer us with awesome truths and righteousness, I God of our salvation, Who are the trust of all men, who dwell at the ends of the earth and of the distant seas.

Verse six

The LORD's creative power is manifested in all the areas of the Universe. His creative power also established the natural forces of nature.

He Who sets fast the mountains with His strength is also girded with victorious might.

Verse seven

David praises the LORD's omnipotent powers. The forces of nature on Earth demonstrate this power.

He stills the roaring of the seas, the roaring of their waves, and also the surging multitude of the peoples;

Verse eight

The Gentiles of the Earth need to acquire a reverence of the LORD. They can acquire this through the signs of the LORD's power. The LORD demonstrates His power every day.

But when the inhabitants of the most distant nations shall have learned to revere You through Your signs, You will make the goings-out of morning and evening to rejoice.

Verse nine

David elaborates upon the way to obtain the salvation which every human can achieve. They must come into the House of the LORD and follow His Laws.

You remembered the earth when You let it languish; You remain in exceedingly great abundance to it; the fountain of God is always filled with water; You will prepare their grain when You will prepare the earth thus.

Verse ten

Water its ridges now, settle down its furrows, make it soft with showers, and bless its growth.

Verse eleven

שְׁנָת (sh'nat) - means "year." The context of the word in this Psalm indicates a new period of time. It is not limited to one year.

Then you have crowned the new era (the year) of Your goodness, and the circles around you drip with abundance.

Verse twelve

The pastures of the desert drip, and the hills gird themselves with joy.

Verse thirteen

יִתְרוֹעֲעוּ (yeet'roaoo) – means "joy." In the context of this Psalm it also means lofty emotions that are expressed in songs and rejoicing.

The meadows clothe themselves with sheep, and valleys cover themselves with grain; they fill themselves with the homage of God; indeed they sing songs beholding His greatness.

Complete Psalm Rewrite Emphasizing Spiritual Awareness

Peace of soul is an emanation of Your mighty acts, O God in Zion, and unto you the vow is made.

Of You Who hears prayer! One day all those that can feel will come unto You. The products of sin that are our common defection have overcome me; You will grant them atonement.

For only he whom You will choose and will bring near unto You strides forward to salvation, so that he may find a dwelling place in You courts. We too wish to be satisfied by the goodness of Your House, which is sanctified in the Abode of your might.

You answer us with awesome truths and righteousness, I God of our salvation, Who are the trust of all men, who dwell at the ends of the earth and of the distant seas.

He Who sets fast the mountains with His strength is also girded with victorious might.

He stills the roaring of the seas, the roaring of their waves, and also the surging multitude of the peoples;

But when the inhabitants of the most distant nations shall have learned to revere You through Your signs, You will make the goings-out of morning and evening to rejoice.

You remembered the earth when You let it languish; You remain in exceedingly great abundance to it; the fountain of God is always filled with water; You will prepare their grain when You will prepare the earth thus.

Water its ridges now, settle down its furrows, make it soft with showers, and bless its growth.

Then you have crowned the new era (the year) of Your goodness, and the circles around you drip with abundance.

The pastures of the desert drip, and the hills gird themselves with joy.

The meadows clothe themselves with sheep, and valleys cover themselves with grain; they fill themselves with the homage of God; indeed they sing songs beholding His greatness.

Psalm 66

New American Standard 1995	Hebrew

Psa. 66:0   For the choir director. A Song. A Psalm.

Psa. 66:1   [a]Shout joyfully to God, all the earth;
2   Sing the [a]glory of His name;
Make His [b]praise glorious.
3   Say to God, "How [a]awesome are Your works!
Because of the greatness of Your power Your enemies will [1b]give feigned obedience to You.
4   "[a]All the earth will worship You,
And will [b]sing praises to You;
They will sing praises to Your name."   [1]Selah.

Psa. 66:5   [a]Come and see the works of God,
Who is [b]awesome in *His* deeds toward the sons of men.
6   He [a]turned the sea into dry land;
They passed through [b]the river on foot;
There let us [c]rejoice in Him!
7   He [a]rules by His might forever;
His [b]eyes keep watch on the nations;
Let not the rebellious [c]exalt themselves. Selah.

Psa. 66:8   Bless our God, O peoples,
And [1a]sound His praise abroad,
9   Who [1a]keeps us in life
And [b]does not allow our feet to [2]slip.

לַמְנַצֵּחַ שִׁיר מִזְמוֹר **Psa. 66:1**
הָרִיעוּ לֵאלֹהִים כָּל־הָאָרֶץ:
2 זַמְּרוּ כְבוֹד־שְׁמוֹ שִׂימוּ
כָבוֹד תְּהִלָּתוֹ: 3 אִמְרוּ
לֵאלֹהִים מַה־נּוֹרָא מַעֲשֶׂיךָ
בְּרֹב עֻזְּךָ יְכַחֲשׁוּ לְךָ
אֹיְבֶיךָ: 4 כָּל־הָאָרֶץ |
יִשְׁתַּחֲווּ לְךָ וִיזַמְּרוּ־לָךְ
יְזַמְּרוּ שִׁמְךָ סֶלָה: 5 לְכוּ
וּרְאוּ מִפְעֲלוֹת אֱלֹהִים נוֹרָא
עֲלִילָה עַל־בְּנֵי אָדָם: 6
הָפַךְ יָם | לְיַבָּשָׁה בַּנָּהָר
יַעַבְרוּ בְרָגֶל שָׁם נִשְׂמְחָה־
בּוֹ: 7 מֹשֵׁל בִּגְבוּרָתוֹ | עוֹלָם
עֵינָיו בַּגּוֹיִם תִּצְפֶּינָה
הַסּוֹרְרִים | אַל־יָרִימוּ
[יָרוּמוּ] לָמוֹ סֶלָה: 8 בָּרְכוּ
עַמִּים | אֱלֹהֵינוּ וְהַשְׁמִיעוּ
קוֹל תְּהִלָּתוֹ: 9 הַשָּׂם נַפְשֵׁנוּ
בַּחַיִּים וְלֹא־נָתַן לַמּוֹט

10 For You have [a]tried us, O God;
You have [b]refined us as silver is refined.
11 You [a]brought us into the net;
You laid an oppressive burden upon our loins.
12 You made men [a]ride over our heads;
We went through [b]fire and through water,
Yet You [c]brought us out into *a place of* abundance.
13 I shall [a]come into Your house with burnt offerings;
I shall [b]pay You my vows,
14 Which my lips uttered
And my mouth spoke when I was [a]in distress.
15 I shall [a]offer to You burnt offerings of fat beasts,
With the smoke of [b]rams;
I shall make *an offering of* [1]bulls with male goats. Selah.

Psa. 66:16 [a]Come *and* hear, all who [1]fear God,
And I will [b]tell of what He has done for my soul.
17 I cried to Him with my mouth,
And [1]He was [a]extolled with my tongue.
18 If I [1a]regard wickedness in my heart,
The [b]Lord [2]will not [3]hear;
19 But certainly [a]God has heard;
He has given heed to the voice of my prayer.
20 [a]Blessed be God,
Who [b]has not turned away my prayer
Nor His lovingkindness from me.

רַגְלֵֽנוּ׃ 10 כִּֽי־בְחַנְתָּ֥נוּ
אֱלֹהִ֑ים צְרַפְתָּ֗נוּ כִּצְרָף־
כָּֽסֶף׃ 11 הֲבֵאתָ֥נוּ בַמְּצוּדָ֑ה
שַׂ֥מְתָּ מוּעָקָ֣ה בְמָתְנֵֽינוּ׃ 12
הִרְכַּ֥בְתָּ אֱנ֗וֹשׁ לְרֹאשֵׁ֫נוּ
בָּֽאנוּ־בָאֵ֥שׁ וּבַמַּ֑יִם וַ֝תּוֹצִיאֵ֗נוּ
לָֽרְוָיָֽה׃ 13 אָב֣וֹא בֵיתְךָ֣
בְעוֹל֑וֹת אֲשַׁלֵּ֖ם לְךָ֣ נְדָרָֽי׃ 14
אֲשֶׁר־פָּצ֥וּ שְׂפָתָ֑י וְדִבֶּר־פִּ֝י
בַּצַּר־לִֽי׃ 15 עֹ֘ל֤וֹת מֵחִ֣ים
אַֽעֲלֶה־לָּ֭ךְ עִם־קְטֹ֣רֶת
אֵילִ֑ים אֶֽעֱשֶׂ֨ה בָקָ֖ר עִם־
עַתּוּדִ֣ים סֶֽלָה׃ 16 לְכֽוּ־שִׁמְע֣וּ
וַֽאֲסַפְּרָ֑ה כָּל־יִרְאֵ֥י אֱלֹהִ֗ים
אֲשֶׁ֖ר עָשָׂ֣ה לְנַפְשִֽׁי׃ 17 אֵלָ֥יו
פִּֽי־קָרָ֑אתִי וְ֝רוֹמַ֗ם תַּ֣חַת
לְשׁוֹנִֽי׃ 18 אָ֭וֶן אִם־רָאִ֣יתִי
בְלִבִּ֑י לֹ֖א יִשְׁמַ֣ע ׀ אֲדֹנָֽי׃ 19
אָכֵ֣ן שָׁמַ֣ע אֱלֹהִ֑ים הִ֝קְשִׁ֗יב
בְּק֣וֹל תְּפִלָּתִֽי׃ 20 בָּר֥וּךְ
אֱלֹהִ֑ים אֲשֶׁ֥ר לֹֽא־הֵסִ֥יר
תְּ֝פִלָּתִ֗י וְחַסְדּ֥וֹ מֵֽאִתִּֽי׃

References

Psalm 66:1
[a]Ps 81:1; 95:1; 98:4; 100:1

Psalm 66:2
[a]Ps 79:9; Is 42:8
[b]Is 42:12

Psalm 66:3
[1]Lit *deceive*
[a]Ps 47:2; 65:5; 145:6
[b]Ps 18:44; 81:15

Psalm 66:4
[1]*Selah* may mean: *Pause, Crescendo* or *Musical interlude*
[a]Ps 22:27; 67:7; 86:9; 117:1; Zech 14:16
[b]Ps 67:4

Psalm 66:5
[a]Ps 46:8
[b]Ps 106:22

Psalm 66:6
[a]Ex 14:21; Ps 106:9
[b]Josh 3:16; Ps 114:3
[c]Ps 105:43

Psalm 66:7
[a]Ps 145:13
[b]Ps 11:4
[c]Ps 140:8

Psalm 66:8
[1]Lit *cause to hear the sound of His praise*
[a]Ps 98:4

Psalm 66:9
[1]Lit *puts our soul in life*
[2]Or *dodder, stumble*

[a]Ps 30:3
[b]Ps 121:3

Psalm 66:10
[a]Job 23:10; Ps 7:9; 17:3; 26:2
[b]Is 48:10; Zech 13:9; Mal 3:3; 1 Pet 1:7

Psalm 66:11
[a]Lam 1:13; Ezek 12:13

Psalm 66:12
[a]Is 51:23
[b]Ps 78:21; Is 43:2
[c]Ps 18:19

Psalm 66:13
[a]Ps 96:8; Jer 17:26
[b]Ps 22:25; 116:14; Eccl 5:4

Psalm 66:14
[a]Ps 18:6

Psalm 66:15
[1]Or *cattle*
[a]Ps 51:19
[b]Num 6:14

Psalm 66:16
[1]Or *revere*
[a]Ps 34:11
[b]Ps 71:15, 24

Psalm 66:17
[1]Or *praise was under my tongue*
[a]Ps 30:1

Psalm 66:18
[1]Or *had regarded*
[2]Or *would*
[3]Or *have heard*
[a]Job 36:21; John 9:31

[b]Job 27:9; Ps 18:41; Prov 1:28; 28:9; Is 1:15; James 4:3

Psalm 66:19
[a]Ps 18:6; 116:1, 2

Psalm 66:20
[a]Ps 68:35
[b]Ps 22:24

Targum

Psa. 66:1 For praise. A praise song. Shout for joy in the presence of the LORD, all inhabitants of the earth. ² Praise the glory of his name; set forth the glory of his praise. ³ Say in the presence of God, "How fearful are your works! For all the abundance of your works, your enemies will deny you." ⁴ All the inhabitants of the earth will bow down before you, and they will praise you, they will praise your name forever. ⁵ Come and see the works of God; fearful is the lord of destiny to the sons of men. ⁶ He turned the Red Sea to dry land; the sons of Israel crossed the river Jordan on their feet; he conveyed them to his holy mountain; there will we rejoice in his word. ⁷ He who rules over the world in the power of his strength, his eyes behold, the Gentiles; let the disobedient not exalt themselves forever. ⁸ Bless God, O Gentiles, and make the sound of his praise heard. ⁹ Who has designated our souls for the life of the age to come, and has not allowed our feet to be shaken. ¹⁰ For you have tried us, O God, you have refined us like a smith who refines silver. [ANOTHER TARGUM: For you have tried [us], for you have tested our fathers, O God; you exiled them among the kingdoms; you found them refined as one who purifies silver.] ¹¹ You brought us into the net, you placed chains on our loins. [ANOTHER TARGUM: You brought us into Egypt as into a net; you placed the rule of the Babylonians upon us, and we became like one on whose loins chains of trouble are placed.] ¹² You humbled us, you made our creditors ride over our heads; you judged us as if by fire and water, and you brought us out to a broad place. [ANOTHER TARGUM: The Medes and Greeks rode over us, they passed over our heads; you brought us among the Romans, who judge us like the cruel Chaldeans, who cast our father Abraham into the fiery furnace, and the Egyptians, who cast our infants into the water; yet you brought us up to freedom.] ¹³ I will enter your house with burnt-offerings, I will pay you my vows. [ANOTHER TARGUM: Just as you have mercy on us and redeem us, then we will enter your sanctuary with burnt-offerings and we will pay you our vows.] ¹⁴ Which opened my lips, and my mouth spoke, when I was in distress. ¹⁵ Fat burnt-offerings I will offer in your presence, with the sweet smell of the sacrifice of rams; I will make [sacrifice of] bulls with he-goats forever. ¹⁶ Come hear, and I will tell all who fear God what he has done for my soul. ¹⁷ I cried out to him with my mouth, and his praise was on my tongue. ¹⁸ If I saw falsehood in my heart, would the LORD not hear? ¹⁹ Truly, God has heard, he listened to the sound of my prayer. ²⁰ Blessed be God, who has not removed my prayer and his favor from me.

Spiritual Awareness

Introduction

David composed this Psalm near the end of his life. Now that peace existed in his kingdom he was free to dream of the Messianic future for his people. The first part of the Psalm deals with past events. Then the Psalm turns to the LORD's redemption of Israel.

Superscript and Verse one

David calls upon the world's nations to acknowledge the LORD's greatness through the manifestations that the LORD has done.

To the Sefirah Netzach who grants victory, a song, a psalm. Waken homage to God of all the Earth.

Verse two

Sing praises of the glory of His Name, and make all glorious things praise His mighty acts.

Verse three

David calls the reader's attention to the acts of the LORD on earth.

Say unto God, What an awesome thing are your Acts, Your enemies feign homage to You through the greatness of Your invincibility.

Verse four

One day humanity will recognize the overpowering majesty of the LORD.

But all the earth shall bow down before You and sing Your praises; they shall sing praises to your name. Meditate on this Verse.

Verse five

The LORD demonstrated his Ways and His sovereignty throughout the history of Israel. By examining and learning about Israel, one can learn about how the LORD works in His creation.

Go and see the works of God; He is awesome in His acts above the sons of man.

Verse six

The event of the Red Sea is remembered because it demonstrated to Israel how much the LORD loves His people.

He has turned the sea into dry land; they passed through the river on foot; there we rejoiced in Him.

Verse seven

The idea of monotheism in David's day is seen in this verse.

Thus, He rules forever in His victorious might; His eyes look around among the nations; let not the disobedient exalt themselves. Meditate upon this verse.

Verse eight

David believed that the LORD was with him because of the victories and other prosperities that the nation enjoyed.

Bless our God, O peoples, and loudly proclaim the praise of His mighty acts.

Verse nine

David believed that the people of Israel were the immortal people among the nations. History proves that the LORD never allowed any nation to destroy Israel. Many have tried over the centuries.

That it is He Who has set up our soul in life and has not allowed our foot to be moved.

Verse ten

The LORD cleansed Israel in David's day.

For you, O God, have tried us; You have refined us even as silver is refined.

Verse eleven

בַּמְצוּדָה (bam'tzooda) means "net prey." This was Israel's political position in the world throughout history. They were a nation isolated from the rest of the world. The nation thought of itself as being captured in a cage.

You brought us into a cage; You imposed constraint upon our loins.

Verse twelve

The Hebrew says that the LORD caused men to ride over Israel in order to keep the people in line. Rabbi Hirsch says that these men were of the lowest class of men in the world. He used the word "rabble" to describe them. The people prayed to the LORD to stop the rabble. This verse could be a description of the Babylonian Exile.

You have caused the rabble to ride over our heads; we were forced to go through fire and water – and then You led us out into abundance.

Verses thirteen and fourteen

These two verses tell us that the Israelites in Babylon craved to go home. Upon returning to Jerusalem they wanted to enter the LORD's home with offerings. Unfortunately, they would have to rebuild the LORD's Temple. David had prophesized the Exile but not the destruction of the Temple. It would have been difficult for him to accept that the Temple where he was collecting building materials would one day be destroyed because of the sins of his descendants.

But I shall come into Your House with ascent-offerings; I will perform my vows unto You;

That which my lips have uttered and my mouth has spoken when distress was mine.

Verse fifteen

This verse is a more detailed description of what was brought as an ascent offering. This is the rule of Hillel. Many Christian interpreters would read this verse as parallel to the preceding two. However, Hillel taught that what appears as a parallel verse expands the first.

I shall bring You ascent offerings of marrow-filled animals with the sweet smoke of rams; I will offer bullocks with goats. Meditate on this Verse.

Verse sixteen

Go and harken, all of you who fear God, so that I may tell what He has done for my soul.

Verse seventeen

This is the psalmist calling out for help from the LORD.

My mouth had cried unto Him, and exaltation was already beneath my tongue.

Verse eighteen, nineteen, and twenty

Had I discerned abuse in my heart, my Master would not have heard me.

But God has heard; He has attended to the voice of my prayer.

Blessed be God, Who has let neither my prayer nor His lovingkindness from the Sefirah Chesed depart from me.

Complete Psalm Rewrite Emphasizing Spiritual Awareness

To the Sefirah Netzach who grants victory, a song, a psalm. Waken homage to God of all the Earth.

Sing praises of the glory of His Name, and make all glorious things praise His mighty acts.

Say unto God, What an awesome thing are your Acts, Your enemies feign homage to You through the greatness of Your invincibility.

But all the earth shall bow down before You and sing Your praises; they shall sing praises to your name. Meditate on this verse.

Go and see the works of God; He is awesome in His acts above the sons of man.

He has turned the sea into dry land; they passed through the river on foot; there we rejoiced in Him.

Thus, He rules forever in His victorious might; His eyes look around among the nations; let not the disobedient exalt themselves. Meditate upon this verse.

Bless our God, O peoples, and loudly proclaim the praise of His mighty acts.

That it is He Who has set up our soul in life and has not allowed our foot to be moved.

For you, O God, have tried us; You have refined us even as silver is refined.

You brought us into a cage; You imposed constraint upon our loins.

You have caused the rabble to ride over our heads; we were forced to go through fire and water – and then You led us out into abundance.

But I shall come into Your House with ascent-offerings; I will perform my vows unto You;

That which my lips have uttered and my mouth has spoken when distress was mine.

I shall bring You ascent offerings of marrow-filled animals with the sweet smoke of rams; I will offer bullocks with goats. Meditate on this Verse.

Go and harken, all of you who fear God, so that I may tell what He has done for my soul.

My mouth had cried unto Him, and exaltation was already beneath my tongue.

Had I discerned abuse in my heart, my Master would not have heard me.

But God has heard; He has attended to the voice of my prayer.

Blessed be God, Who has let neither my prayer nor His lovingkindness from the Sefirah Chesed depart from me.

Psalm 67

New American Standard 1995	Hebrew
Psa. 67:0 For the choir director; with stringed instruments. A Psalm. A Song.	**Psa. 67:1** לַמְנַצֵּחַ בִּנְגִינֹת
Psa. 67:1 God be gracious to us and [a]bless us, *And* [b]cause His face to shine [1]upon us — [2]Selah.	מִזְמוֹר שִׁיר ׃ 2 אֱלֹהִים יְחָנֵּנוּ וִיבָרְכֵנוּ יָאֵר פָּנָיו אִתָּנוּ
2 That [a]Your way may be known on the earth, [b]Your salvation among all nations.	סֶלָה ׃ 3 לָדַעַת בָּאָרֶץ דַּרְכֶּךָ בְּכָל־גּוֹיִם יְשׁוּעָתֶךָ ׃ 4 יוֹדוּךָ
3 Let the [a]peoples praise You, O God; Let all the peoples praise You.	עַמִּים ׀ אֱלֹהִים יוֹדוּךָ עַמִּים
4 Let the [a]nations be glad and sing for joy; For You will [b]judge the peoples with uprightness And [c]guide the nations on the earth. Selah.	כֻּלָּם ׃ 5 יִשְׂמְחוּ וִירַנְּנוּ לְאֻמִּים כִּי־תִשְׁפֹּט עַמִּים מִישׁוֹר וּלְאֻמִּים ׀ בָּאָרֶץ
5 Let the [a]peoples praise You, O God; Let all the peoples praise You.	תַּנְחֵם סֶלָה ׃ 6 יוֹדוּךָ עַמִּים ׀
6 The [a]earth has yielded its produce; God, our God, [b]blesses us.	אֱלֹהִים יוֹדוּךָ עַמִּים כֻּלָּם ׃ 7 אֶרֶץ נָתְנָה יְבוּלָהּ יְבָרְכֵנוּ
7 God blesses us, [1]That [a]all the ends of the earth may fear Him.	אֱלֹהִים אֱלֹהֵינוּ ׃ 8 יְבָרְכֵנוּ אֱלֹהִים וְיִירְאוּ אֹתוֹ כָּל־אַפְסֵי־אָרֶץ ׃

References

Psalm 67:1
[1]Lit *with*
[2]*Selah* may mean: *Pause, Crescendo* or *Musical interlude*
[a]Num 6:25
[b]Ps 4:6; 31:16; 80:3, 7, 19; 119:135

Psalm 67:2
[a]Ps 98:2; Acts 18:25; Titus 2:11
[b]Is 52:10

Psalm 67:3
[a]Ps 66:4

Psalm 67:4
[a]Ps 100:1, 2
[b]Ps 9:8; 96:10, 13; 98:9
[c]Ps 47:8

Psalm 67:5
[a]Ps 67:3

Psalm 67:6
[a]Lev 26:4; Ps 85:12; Ezek 34:27; Zech 8:12
[b]Ps 29:11; 115:12

Psalm 67:7
[1]Or *And let all...earth fear Him*
[a]Ps 22:27; 33:8

Targum

Psa. 67:1 For praise, with melodies; a psalm and a song. [2] God will pity us and bless us; he will make the splendor of his face shine on us forever. [3] To make known your way in the land, your redemption among all the Gentiles. [4] The Gentiles will give thanks in your presence, O God, all the Gentiles will give thanks. [5] The nations will rejoice and exult, for you will judge the peoples with honesty, and you will guide the nations in the land forever. [6] The peoples will give thanks in your presence, O God, all the peoples will give thanks. [7] The land has given its fruit; God, our God, will bless us. [8] God will bless us, and all the ends of the earth will fear him.

Spiritual Awareness

Introduction

This Psalm is extraordinary that it was revealed to Moses and David. This Psalm is considered a holy vision. The Psalm was engraved on a sheet of the purest gold. It was fashioned in the shape of a seven-branched candelabrum. Tradition says that David engraved this Psalm on his shield so that he could study it before going into battle.

Superscript

To the Sefirah Netzach, who grants victory through the power of music. A Psalm, a song.

Verse one

The request is for intellectual abilities to be able to know the LORD. We ask the LORD to make known the goals of His ways. The presence of the LORD is with us through His Shekinah. People want that feeling, but also, the purpose the LORD has for us is crucial.

May God grant us spiritual gifts and bless us, and make His countenance shine among us. Meditate on this verse.

Verse two

לָדַעַת (ladaat) – means "to know." Daat is the name of the quasi-Sefirah, which Rabbi Lauri said is the combination of Keter, Chochmah, and Binah. Daat is also referred to as the God-head. Knowledge combines the spiritual attributes of the top three Sefirah of the Tree of Life. The Psalmist calls out to Daat to determine what the God-head intentions are.

Daat make known Your way on earth, Your salvation among all nations.

Verse three

The LORD knew that at first, only a few of the world's peoples would turn to Him, but eventually, all the peoples of the earth would come to worship the LORD.

So that the nations shall render You homage, O God; all the nations shall render You homage one day.

Verse four

The people will turn to the LORD, and their leaders will worship You.

The nations will be glad and rejoice, for You will range the peoples in order and will lead the nations upon earth. Meditate upon this verse.

Verses five through seven

Eventually, the leaders of the nations will withdraw entirely from their positions of power because the nations will render homage to the LORD and will not need an intermediary.

Then the peoples shall render homage to God; the peoples shall all render homage to You.

Then the earth shall have yielded its produce, and God, our own God, shall bless us henceforth.

God shall bless us, and all the ends of the earth shall reverently fear Him.

Complete Psalm Rewrite Emphasizing Spiritual Awareness

To the Sefirah Netzach, who grants victory through the power of music. A Psalm, a song.

May God grant us spiritual gifts and bless us, and make His countenance shine among us. Meditate on this verse.

Daat make known Your way on earth, Your salvation among all nations.

So that the nations shall render You homage, O God; all the nations shall render You homage one day

The nations will be glad and rejoice, for You will range the peoples in order and will lead the nations upon earth. Meditate upon this verse.

Then the peoples shall render homage to God; the peoples shall all render homage to You.

Then the earth shall have yielded its produce, and God, our own God, shall bless us henceforth.

God shall bless us, and all the ends of the earth shall reverently fear Him

Psalm 68

New American Standard 1995	Hebrew
Psa. 68:0 For the choir director. A Psalm of David. A Song. **Psa. 68:1** [1]Let [a]God arise, [2]let His enemies be scattered, And [3]let those who hate Him flee before Him. 2 As [a]smoke is driven away, *so drive them* away; As [b]wax melts before the fire, *So* let the [c]wicked perish before God. 3 But let the [a]righteous be glad; let them exult before God; Yes, let them rejoice with gladness. 4 Sing to God, [a]sing praises to His name; [1b]Lift up *a song* for Him who [c]rides through the deserts, Whose [d]name is [2]the LORD, and exult before Him. **Psa. 68:5** A [a]father of the fatherless and a [b]judge [1]for the widows, Is God in His [c]holy habitation. 6 God [1a]makes a home for the lonely; He [b]leads out the prisoners into prosperity, Only [c]the rebellious dwell in a parched land. **Psa. 68:7** O God, when You [a]went forth before Your people,	לַמְנַצֵּחַ לְדָוִד מִזְמוֹר **Psa. 68:1** שִׁיר : [2] יָקוּם אֱלֹהִים יָפוּצוּ אוֹיְבָיו וְיָנוּסוּ מְשַׂנְאָיו מִפָּנָיו : [3] כְּהִנְדֹּף עָשָׁן תִּנְדֹּף כְּהִמֵּס דּוֹנַג מִפְּנֵי־אֵשׁ יֹאבְדוּ רְשָׁעִים מִפְּנֵי אֱלֹהִים : [4] וְצַדִּיקִים יִשְׂמְחוּ יַעַלְצוּ לִפְנֵי אֱלֹהִים וְיָשִׂישׂוּ בְשִׂמְחָה : [5] שִׁירוּ לֵאלֹהִים זַמְּרוּ שְׁמוֹ סֹלּוּ לָרֹכֵב בָּעֲרָבוֹת בְּיָהּ שְׁמוֹ וְעִלְזוּ לְפָנָיו : [6] אֲבִי יְתוֹמִים וְדַיַּן אַלְמָנוֹת אֱלֹהִים בִּמְעוֹן קָדְשׁוֹ : [7] אֱלֹהִים מוֹשִׁיב יְחִידִים בַּיְתָה מוֹצִיא אֲסִירִים בַּכּוֹשָׁרוֹת אַךְ סוֹרְרִים שָׁכְנוּ צְחִיחָה : [8] אֱלֹהִים בְּצֵאתְךָ לִפְנֵי עַמֶּךָ בְּצַעְדְּךָ בִישִׁימוֹן סֶלָה : [9] אֶרֶץ רָעָשָׁה אַף־שָׁמַיִם

When You [b]marched through the wilderness,   [1]Selah.

8   The [a]earth quaked;

The [b]heavens also dropped *rain* at the presence of God;

[1c]Sinai itself *quaked* at the presence of God, the God of Israel.

9   You [a]shed abroad a plentiful rain, O God;

You confirmed Your inheritance when it was [1]parched.

10   Your creatures settled in it;

You [a]provided in Your goodness for the poor, O God.

Psa. 68:11   The Lord gives the [1]command;

The [a]women who proclaim the *good* tidings are a great host:

12   "[a]Kings of armies flee, they flee,

And she who remains at home will [b]divide the spoil!"

13   [1]When you lie down [a]among the [2]sheepfolds,

You are like the wings of a dove covered with silver,

And its pinions with glistening gold.

14   When the Almighty [a]scattered the kings [1]there,

It was snowing in [b]Zalmon.

Psa. 68:15   A [1a]mountain of God is the mountain of Bashan;

A mountain *of many* peaks is the mountain of Bashan.

16   Why do you look with envy, O mountains with *many* peaks,

At the mountain which God has [a]desired for His abode?

נָטְפוּ מִפְּנֵי אֱלֹהִים זֶה סִינַי
מִפְּנֵי אֱלֹהִים אֱלֹהֵי יִשְׂרָאֵל:

10 גֶּשֶׁם נְדָבוֹת תָּנִיף אֱלֹהִים
נַחֲלָתְךָ וְנִלְאָה אַתָּה
כוֹנַנְתָּהּ: 11 חַיָּתְךָ יָשְׁבוּ־בָהּ
תָּכִין בְּטוֹבָתְךָ לֶעָנִי
אֱלֹהִים: 12 אֲדֹנָי יִתֶּן־אֹמֶר
הַמְבַשְּׂרוֹת צָבָא רָב: 13
מַלְכֵי צְבָאוֹת יִדֹּדוּן יִדֹּדוּן
וּנְוַת בַּיִת תְּחַלֵּק שָׁלָל: 14
אִם־תִּשְׁכְּבוּן בֵּין שְׁפַתָּיִם
כַּנְפֵי יוֹנָה נֶחְפָּה בַכֶּסֶף
וְאֶבְרוֹתֶיהָ בִּירַקְרַק חָרוּץ:
15 בְּפָרֵשׂ שַׁדַּי מְלָכִים בָּהּ
תַּשְׁלֵג בְּצַלְמוֹן: 16 הַר־
אֱלֹהִים הַר־בָּשָׁן הַר גַּבְנֻנִּים
הַר־בָּשָׁן: 17 לָמָּה תְּרַצְּדוּן
הָרִים גַּבְנֻנִּים הָהָר חָמַד
אֱלֹהִים לְשִׁבְתּוֹ אַף־יְהוָה
יִשְׁכֹּן לָנֶצַח: 18 רֶכֶב אֱלֹהִים
רִבֹּתַיִם אַלְפֵי שִׁנְאָן אֲדֹנָי
בָם סִינַי בַּקֹּדֶשׁ: 19 עָלִיתָ
לַמָּרוֹם שָׁבִיתָ שֶּׁבִי לָקַחְתָּ

Surely *b*the LORD will dwell *there* forever.

17   The *a*chariots of God are [1]myriads, *b*thousands upon thousands;

[2]The Lord is among them *as at* Sinai, in holiness.

18   You have *a*ascended on high, You have *b*led captive *Your* captives;

You have received gifts among men,

Even *among* the rebellious also, that [1]the LORD God may dwell *there*.

Psa. 68:19   Blessed be the Lord, who daily *a*bears our burden,

*b*The God *who* is our Salvation. Selah.

20   God is to us a *a*God of deliverances;

And *b*to [1]GOD the Lord belong escapes [2]from death.

21   Surely God will *a*shatter the head of His enemies,

The hairy crown of him who goes on in his guilty deeds.

22   The Lord [1]said, "*a*I will bring *them* back from Bashan.

I will bring *them* back from the depths of the sea;

23   That [1a]your foot may shatter *them* in blood,

The tongue of your *b*dogs *may have* its portion from *your* enemies."

Psa. 68:24   They have seen *a*Your [1]procession, O God,

The [1]procession of my God, my King, [2b]into the sanctuary.

25   The *a*singers went on, the musicians after *them*,

מַתָּנוֹת בָּאָדָם וְאַף סוֹרְרִים לִשְׁכֹּן ׀ יָהּ אֱלֹהִים׃ 20 בָּרוּךְ אֲדֹנָי יוֹם ׀ יוֹם יַעֲמָס־לָנוּ הָאֵל יְשׁוּעָתֵנוּ סֶלָה׃ 21 הָאֵל ׀ לָנוּ אֵל לְמוֹשָׁעוֹת וְלֵיהוִה אֲדֹנָי לַמָּוֶת תּוֹצָאוֹת׃ 22 אַךְ־אֱלֹהִים יִמְחַץ רֹאשׁ אֹיְבָיו קָדְקֹד שֵׂעָר מִתְהַלֵּךְ בַּאֲשָׁמָיו׃ 23 אָמַר אֲדֹנָי מִבָּשָׁן אָשִׁיב אָשִׁיב מִמְּצֻלוֹת יָם׃ 24 לְמַעַן ׀ תִּמְחַץ רַגְלְךָ בְּדָם לְשׁוֹן כְּלָבֶיךָ מֵאֹיְבִים מִנֵּהוּ׃ 25 רָאוּ הֲלִיכוֹתֶיךָ אֱלֹהִים הֲלִיכוֹת אֵלִי מַלְכִּי בַקֹּדֶשׁ׃ 26 קִדְּמוּ שָׁרִים אַחַר נֹגְנִים בְּתוֹךְ עֲלָמוֹת תּוֹפֵפוֹת׃ 27 בְּמַקְהֵלוֹת בָּרְכוּ אֱלֹהִים יְהוָה מִמְּקוֹר יִשְׂרָאֵל׃ 28 שָׁם בִּנְיָמִן ׀ צָעִיר רֹדֵם שָׂרֵי יְהוּדָה רִגְמָתָם שָׂרֵי זְבֻלוּן שָׂרֵי נַפְתָּלִי׃ 29 צִוָּה אֱלֹהֶיךָ עֻזֶּךָ עוּזָּה אֱלֹהִים זוּ פָּעַלְתָּ לָּנוּ׃ 30

[1]In the midst of the [b]maidens beating tambourines.

26 [a]Bless God in the congregations,
Even the LORD, *you who are* of the [b]fountain of Israel.

27 There is [a]Benjamin, the [1]youngest, [2]ruling them,
The princes of Judah *in their* throng,
The princes of [b]Zebulun, the princes of Naphtali.

Psa. 68:28   [1]Your God has [a]commanded your strength;
Show Yourself strong, O God, [b]who have acted [2]on our behalf.

29 [1]Because of Your temple at Jerusalem
[a]Kings will bring gifts to You.

30 Rebuke the [a]beasts [1]in the reeds,
The herd of [b]bulls with the calves of the peoples,
Trampling under foot the pieces of silver;
He has [c]scattered the peoples who delight in war.

31 Envoys will come out of [a]Egypt;
[1b]Ethiopia will quickly stretch out her hands to God.

Psa. 68:32   Sing to God, O [a]kingdoms of the earth,
[b]Sing praises to the Lord, Selah.

33 To Him who [a]rides upon the [1b]highest heavens, which are from ancient times;
Behold, [c]He [2]speaks forth with His voice, a [d]mighty voice.

34 [a]Ascribe strength to God;
His majesty is over Israel
And [b]His strength is in the [1]skies.

מֵהֵיכָלֶךָ עַל־יְרוּשָׁלִַם לְךָ
יוֹבִילוּ מְלָכִים שָׁי ׃ 31 גְּעַר
חַיַּת קָנֶה עֲדַת אַבִּירִים |
בְּעֶגְלֵי עַמִּים מִתְרַפֵּס
בְּרַצֵּי־כָסֶף בִּזַּר עַמִּים
קְרָבוֹת יֶחְפָּצוּ ׃ 32 יֶאֱתָיוּ
חַשְׁמַנִּים מִנִּי מִצְרָיִם כּוּשׁ
תָּרִיץ יָדָיו לֵאלֹהִים ׃ 33
מַמְלְכוֹת הָאָרֶץ שִׁירוּ
לֵאלֹהִים זַמְּרוּ אֲדֹנָי סֶלָה ׃
34 לָרֹכֵב בִּשְׁמֵי שְׁמֵי־קֶדֶם הֵן
יִתֵּן בְּקוֹלוֹ קוֹל עֹז ׃ 35 תְּנוּ עֹז
לֵאלֹהִים עַל־יִשְׂרָאֵל גַּאֲוָתוֹ
וְעֻזּוֹ בַּשְּׁחָקִים ׃ 36 נוֹרָא
אֱלֹהִים מִמִּקְדָּשֶׁיךָ אֵל
יִשְׂרָאֵל הוּא נֹתֵן | עֹז
וְתַעֲצֻמוֹת לָעָם בָּרוּךְ
אֱלֹהִים ׃

<table>
<tr><td>

35 [1]O God, *You are* [a]awesome from Your [2]sanctuary.

The God of Israel Himself [b]gives strength and power to the people.

[c]Blessed be God!

</td><td></td></tr>
</table>

References

Psalm 68:1
[1]Or *God shall*
[2]Or *His enemies shall*
[3]Or *those who hate Him shall*
[a]Num 10:35; Ps 12:5; 132:8

Psalm 68:2
[a]Ps 37:20; Is 9:18; Hos 13:3
[b]Ps 22:14; 97:5; Mic 1:4
[c]Ps 9:3; 37:20; 80:16

Psalm 68:3
[a]Ps 32:11; 64:10; 97:12

Psalm 68:4
[1]Or *Cast up* a highway
[2]Heb *YAH*
[a]Ps 66:2
[b]Is 57:14; 62:10
[c]Deut 33:26; Ps 18:10; 68:33; Is 40:3
[d]Ex 6:3; Ps 83:18

Psalm 68:5
[1]Lit *of*
[a]Ps 10:14; 146:9
[b]Deut 10:18
[c]Deut 26:15

Psalm 68:6
[1]Lit *makes the solitary to dwell in a house*
[a]Ps 107:4-7; 113:9
[b]Ps 69:33; 102:20; 107:10, 14; 146:7; Acts 12:7; 16:26
[c]Ps 78:17; 107:34, 40

Psalm 68:7
[1]*Selah* may mean: *Pause, Crescendo* or *Musical interlude*
[a]Ex 13:21; Ps 78:14; Hab 3:13
[b]Judg 5:4; Ps 78:52

Psalm 68:8
[1]Lit *This is Sinai* which
[a]Ex 19:18; Judg 5:4; 2 Sam 22:8; Ps 77:18; Jer 10:10
[b]Judg 5:4; Ps 18:9; Is 45:8
[c]Ex 19:18; Judg 5:5

Psalm 68:9
[1]Lit *weary*
[a]Lev 26:4; Deut 11:11; Job 5:10; Ezek 34:26

Psalm 68:10
[a]Ps 65:9; 74:19; 78:20; 107:9

Psalm 68:11
[1]Lit *word*
[a]Ex 15:20; 1 Sam 18:6

Psalm 68:12
[a]Josh 10:16; Judg 5:19; Ps 135:11
[b]Judg 5:30; 1 Sam 30:24

Psalm 68:13
[1]Lit *If*
[2]Or *cooking stones* or *saddle bags*
[a]Gen 49:14; Judg 5:16

Psalm 68:14
[1]Lit *in it*
[a]Josh 10:10
[b]Judg 9:48

Psalm 68:15
[1]Or *mighty mountain is*
[a]Ps 36:6

Psalm 68:16
[a]Deut 12:5; Ps 87:1, 2; 132:13
[b]Ps 132:14

Psalm 68:17
[1]Lit *twice ten thousand*

[2]Another reading is *The Lord came from Sinai into the sanctuary*
[a]2 Kin 6:17; Hab 3:8
[b]Deut 33:2; Dan 7:10

Psalm 68:18
[1]Heb *YAH*
[a]Ps 7:7; 47:5; Eph 4:8
[b]Judg 5:12

Psalm 68:19
[a]Ps 55:22; Is 46:4
[b]Ps 65:5

Psalm 68:20
[1]Heb *YHWH,* usually rendered *LORD*
[2]I.e. in view of; lit *for*
[a]Ps 106:43
[b]Deut 32:39; Ps 49:15; 56:13

Psalm 68:21
[a]Ps 110:6; Hab 3:13

Psalm 68:22
[1]Or *says*
[a]Num 21:33; Amos 9:1-3

Psalm 68:23
[1]Some versions render, you may *bathe your foot in blood*
[a]Ps 58:10
[b]1 Kin 21:19; Jer 15:3

Psalm 68:24
[1]Lit *goings*
[2]Lit *in the sanctuary;* or *in holiness*
[a]Ps 77:13
[b]Ps 63:2

Psalm 68:25
[1]Or *The maidens in the midst*
[a]1 Chr 13:8; 15:6; Ps 47:6
[b]Ex 15:20; Judg 11:34

Psalm 68:26
[a]Ps 22:22, 23; 26:12
[b]Deut 33:28; Is 48:1

Psalm 68:27
[1]Or *smallest*
[2]Or *their ruler*
[a]Judg 5:14; 1 Sam 9:21
[b]Judg 5:18

Psalm 68:28
[1]Some mss read *Command, God*
[2]Lit *for us*
[a]Ps 29:11; 44:4
[b]Is 26:12

Psalm 68:29
[1]Or *From Your temple*
[a]1 Kin 10:10, 25; 2 Chr 32:23; Ps 45:12; 72:10; Is 18:7

Psalm 68:30
[1]Lit *of*
[a]Job 40:21; Ezek 29:3
[b]Ps 22:12
[c]Ps 18:14; 89:10

Psalm 68:31
[1]Lit *Cush*
[a]Is 19:19, 21
[b]Is 45:14; Zeph 3:10

Psalm 68:32
[a]Ps 102:22
[b]Ps 67:4

Psalm 68:33
[1]Lit *heaven of heavens of old*
[2]Lit *gives forth*
[a]Deut 33:26; Ps 18:10; 104:3
[b]Deut 10:14; 1 Kin 8:27

[c]Ps 46:6
[d]Ps 29:4

Psalm 68:34
[1]Lit *clouds*
[a]Ps 29:1
[b]Ps 150:1

Psalm 68:35
[1]Or *Awesome is God from your sanctuary*
[2]Lit *holy places*
[a]Deut 7:21; 10:17; Ps 47:2; 66:5
[b]Ps 29:11; Is 40:29
[c]Ps 66:20; 2 Cor 1:3

Targum

Psa. 68:1 For praise, of David. A hymn and song. ² God will arise, his enemies will be scattered, and his foes will flee from his presence. ³ Just as the smoke is driven out, they will be driven; just as wax will melt in the presence of fire, the wicked will perish in the presence of God. ⁴ And the righteous will rejoice and exult in the presence of the LORD, and they will rejoice joyfully. ⁵ Give praise in the presence of God, praise his glorious name; magnify the one who sits on his glorious throne in Araboth; Yah is his name; and be glad in his presence. ⁶ Father of the orphans, and judge of widows – such is God in the dwelling place of his holy presence. ⁷ God, who makes matches, joining the solitary to mates; who brought out the house of Israel, who were bound in Egypt; for the correct deeds of their fathers <he redeemed them> in public procession; but Pharaoh and his armies, who refused to let them go, dwelt in thirst. ⁸ O God, when you went forth in a pillar of cloud and in a pillar of fire before your people, when you traveled in the wilderness of Jeshimon forever, when you gave the Torah to your people – ⁹ The earth shook, also the heavens dropped dew in the presence of the LORD; as for this Sinai, its smoke went up like the smoke of a furnace before the LORD, God of Israel, was manifested upon it. ¹⁰ When the house of Israel heard the voice of your power, their souls flew away; at once he made to descend upon them the dew of resurrection; O God, you brought the favorable rain to your inheritance, and you supported the assembly which was exhausted. ¹¹ You caused your vigor to go back to it; you appointed a troop of angels to do good to the poor of God. ¹² The LORD gave the words of Torah to his people; truly, Moses and Aaron [were] proclaiming the word of God to the great army. ¹³ Kingdoms with their armies went into exile from their palaces, and the wise were exiled from their knowledge; but the assembly of Israel divides the spoil from heaven. ¹⁴ <The God of Israel said:> If you wicked kings lay down among the rubbish heaps, the assembly of Israel, likened to a dove flying in the clouds of glory, divides the spoil of the Egyptians – silver that is refined, and her treasures full of pure gold. [ANOTHER TARGUM: If you wicked kings sleep in the theatres, which are likened to rubbish heaps, behold, the sons of the assembly of Israel, which are likened to the wings of a dove, are covered with the words of Torah, which are likened to silver, and her scholars, which are likened to the pinions of a young dove in pure gold.] ¹⁵ When she spread her hands over the sea in prayer, Shaddai abased kingdoms, and on her account clouded over Gehinnom like snow; he delivered them from the shadow of death. [ANOTHER TARGUM: Because of this, when the priests spread their hands and bless the people of Israel, Shaddai agrees with them and kings are subdued beneath them; and because of their merits, their sins are made white as snow, and Gehinnom is cooled for the wicked who have received punishment in their children and have repented of their bad deeds.] ¹⁶ Mount Moriah, the place where the patriarchs worshipped in the presence of the LORD, was chosen for the building of the sanctuary; and Mount Sinai for the giving of Torah; Mount Mathnan, Mount Tabor, and Carmel were disqualified, and a hump was made for them like Mount Mathnan. [ANOTHER TARGUM: Mount Moriah was chosen first for the worship of the patriarchs in the presence of the LORD, and was chosen second for the building there of the sanctuary; and Mount Sinai was pulled up from there and chosen third for the Torah; Mount Buthnin was removed and set far away; Mount Tabor – a miracle was performed there for Barak and Deborah; Mount Carmel – miracles were performed there for Elijah the prophet. And they were racing, one against the other, and arguing one with the other. One said, "On me the presence shall abide," and the other would say, "On me the presence will abide." And the Lord of the World, who sharpens the proud and rebellious with the humble, struck them down and they were disqualified. A hump was made for them like Mount Buthnin.] [17] God said, Why do you leap, O mountains? It is not my will to give the Torah on proud, contemptuous mountains. Behold, Mount Sinai which is humble; the word of the LORD desires to place his presence upon it; [but] in the highest heaven the LORD will abide forever. [18] The chariots of God are two myriads of burning fire, two thousand angels guiding them; the presence of the LORD rests on them, on the mountain of Sinai, in holiness. [19] You ascended to the firmament, O prophet Moses; you captured captives, you taught the words of Torah, you gave gifts to the sons of men, and even the stubborn who are converted turn in repentance, [and] the glorious presence of the LORD God abides upon them. [20] Blessed be the LORD, every day he weighs us down, adding commandments to commandments; the mighty one, who is our redemption and our helper forever. [21] God is for us might and redemption; and from God the LORD death and loss of breath are inflicted on the wicked through suffocation. [22] Truly, God will break the heads of his enemies, he will make fall out the hair of the man who keeps walking in his sins. [23] The LORD says, "I will bring back the righteous who have died and been eaten by wild beasts from Buthnin; I will bring back the righteous who have drowned in the depths of the sea." [24] So that they will see the punishment of the wicked, they will dip their feet in the blood of the slain; the tongue of the wild beast will grow fat from their plumpness, some of them will be sated on the enemies. [25] The house of Israel has seen the paths of your presence on the sea, O God; they say, "The paths of God, king of all the world in holiness!" [26] They rose up early and uttered a song after Moses and Aaron who were playing melodies before them, in the midst of the righteous women who were with Miriam playing timbrels. [27] In the midst of the assemblies, bless God, exalt the LORD, O fetuses in the bellies of their mothers, O seed of Israel! [28] There Benjamin, least of the tribes, who first of all went into the sea — because of this, he received kingship; and after them went down the princes of Judah; the tribes stoned them with stones, and they received dominion after them; the princes of Zebulun were their merchants, and the princes of Naphtali were their warriors. [29] God has commanded your strength; be strong, O God, abide in this sanctuary you have made for us! [30] From your temple you will accept sacrifices; your presence abides on Jerusalem; from their palaces the kings will bring to you sacrifices. [31] Rebuke the armies of sinners, shatter them like reeds, the assembly of warriors who trust in calves, the idols of the Gentiles. His favor is toward the people who are occupied willingly in the Torah, which is purer than silver. Scatter the peoples who desire to wage war! 32 The children of Ham, the Osmani(?), will come from Egypt to be converted; the children of Cush will run to spread their hands in prayer before God. 33 O kingdoms of the earth, sing praise in the presence of the LORD, sing praise to the LORD forever. 34 To the one who sits on his throne in the heaven of heavens; in the beginning he, by his command, gave through his voice the voice of the spirit of prophecy to the prophets. 35 Ascribe the glory of strength to God, whose excellence is over Israel, and whose strength is in heaven. 36 Fearful is God, from your sanctuary; the mighty one of Israel has given strength and might to his people. Blessed be God!

Spiritual Awareness

Introduction

The theme of this Psalm is the Revelation at Mount Sinai. Israel emerged from this event as the Chosen People of the LORD. At Mount Sinai, the people agreed to be the LORD's people by following His laws. The Ten Commandments is a treaty between God and the people. The LORD would protect the people as long as they followed the Torah. Midrash says that every Jewish soul, past, present, and future, was at Sinai for this event. Therefore, Jews today were at Sinai and must keep the covenant because they were a part of it.

Unfortunately, the world's nations became jealous of Israel both then and now. The world's nations have tried to snuff the Hebrew people out for centuries. However, the LORD promised that a remanent of the people would always remain. From the time of Abraham to the present, the LORD has been with His Chosen People. The dark times of the Babylonian Exile and the Holocaust damaged Israel but never eliminated them. The LORD ensured that the nation was rebuilt every time.

Due to the length of the Psalm, only the spiritual awareness of verses will be explored.

Superscript

To the Sefirah Netzach who grants victory, by David, a Psalm, a song.

Verse two

The lawless are the nations and people who do not want to follow the Torah of the LORD. The LORD will eventually destroy these nations.

But even as smoke, slowly fading, blows away, even as wax melts before the fire, so the lawless shall perish before the presence of God.

Verse four

Even though Israel is the Chosen People, the LORD commands them to show the world what it means to be a people of God. Therefore, they will want to become a part of the covenant. A view of being the Chosen People is that this natoin is to bring the LORD's Torah to the world.

Sing to God, sing praises to His Name, soar up to Him Who guides worlds through barrenness by His Name, and exult greatly before his countenance.

Verse seven

The LORD revealed His power to Israel by leading them from Egypt to Sinai as a cloud during the day and a fire at night.

Thus, O God, when You went forth before Your people, when You marched through the wilderness. Meditate on this verse.

Verse thirteen

Scripture often uses the dove as an allegory of the Jewish nation. In this verse, the dove is in flight, spreading her wings to capture the bright sun's light. Israel always tries to capture the presence of the LORD. It attempts to hear the commandments and directions coming from Heaven.

O, would that you were to remain quietly among the rows of vessels! Even the wing of the dove is covered with silver, and its pinions with sharp gold.

Verse nineteen

The Psalmist writes that the LORD daily bears the burdens of Israel. Israel has been under constant pressure from the world's nations ever since Jacob moved the family to Egypt. The nations of the world desire a closer walk with the LORD but do not follow His Torah and the words of the prophets. It is not an easy life being a devoted Jew. However, in the end, it is more than worth the difficulties.

Blessed be my Master day by day; may He give us a burden to bear. Even the same God is also our Salvation. Meditate on this verse.

Verse twenty-two

"Bashan symbolizes that which is exalted in the flesh, which God's people will conquer as they make their way toward the rest of God. The elect have labored for many centuries in the bondage of spiritual ambition. God will bring His chosen people from the bondage of sin and self-will and establish them on Mount Zion, the place of their true inheritance."[1]

My Master has promised it; I shall bring you back from Bashan, I will bring you back from the shadowy depths of the sea.

Verse thirty-two

The LORD will make His presence known to all the nations of the earth who turn back to Him.

O kingdoms of the earth, sing to God, sing praises to my Master. Meditate on this verse.

---

[1] http://www.wor.org/book/3681/the-mountains-of-bashan. Accessed December 31, 2022.

Psalm 69

New American Standard 1995	Hebrew

Psa. 69:0 For the choir director; according to †Shoshannim. *A Psalm* of David.

Psa. 69:1 Save me, O God,
For the [a]waters have [1]threatened my life.
2 I have sunk in deep [a]mire, and there is no foothold;
I have come into deep waters, and a [1b]flood overflows me.
3 I am [a]weary with my crying; my throat is parched;
My [b]eyes fail while I wait for my God.
4 Those [a]who hate me without a cause are more than the hairs of my head;
Those who would [1]destroy me [b]are powerful, being wrongfully my enemies;
[c]What I did not steal, I then have to restore.

Psa. 69:5 O God, it is You who knows [a]my folly,
And [b]my wrongs are not hidden from You.
6 May those who wait for You not [a]be ashamed through me, O Lord [1]GOD of hosts;
May those who seek You not be dishonored through me, O God of Israel,
7 Because [a]for Your sake I have borne reproach;

Psa. 69:1 לַמְנַצֵּחַ עַל־שׁוֹשַׁנִּים

לְדָוִד ׃ 2 הוֹשִׁיעֵנִי אֱלֹהִים כִּי

3 בָאוּ מַיִם עַד־נָפֶשׁ ׃

טָבַעְתִּי ׀ בִּיוֵן מְצוּלָה וְאֵין

מָעֳמָד בָּאתִי בְמַעֲמַקֵּי־מַיִם

וְשִׁבֹּלֶת שְׁטָפָתְנִי ׃ 4 יָגַעְתִּי

בְקָרְאִי נִחַר גְּרוֹנִי כָּלוּ עֵינַי

מְיַחֵל לֵאלֹהָי ׃ 5 רַבּוּ ׀

מִשַּׂעֲרוֹת רֹאשִׁי שֹׂנְאַי חִנָּם

עָצְמוּ מַצְמִיתַי אֹיְבַי שֶׁקֶר

אֲשֶׁר לֹא־גָזַלְתִּי אָז אָשִׁיב ׃ 6

אֱלֹהִים אַתָּה יָדַעְתָּ לְאִוַּלְתִּי

וְאַשְׁמוֹתַי מִמְּךָ לֹא־נִכְחָדוּ ׃

7 אַל־יֵבֹשׁוּ בִי ׀ קֹוֶיךָ אֲדֹנָי

יְהוִה צְבָאוֹת אַל־יִכָּלְמוּ בִי

8 מְבַקְשֶׁיךָ אֱלֹהֵי יִשְׂרָאֵל ׃

כִּי־עָלֶיךָ נָשָׂאתִי חֶרְפָּה

כִּסְּתָה כְלִמָּה פָנָי ׃ 9 מוּזָר

הָיִיתִי לְאֶחָי וְנָכְרִי לִבְנֵי

אִמִּי ׃ 10 כִּי־קִנְאַת בֵּיתְךָ

[b]Dishonor has covered my face.

8 I have become [a]estranged [1]from my brothers

And an alien to my mother's sons.

9 For [a]zeal for Your house has consumed me,

And [b]the reproaches of those who reproach You have fallen on me.

10 When I wept [a]in my soul with fasting,

It became my reproach.

11 When I made [a]sackcloth my clothing,

I became [b]a byword to them.

12 Those who [a]sit in the gate talk about me,

And I *am* the [1b]song of the drunkards.

Psa. 69:13 But as for me, my prayer is to You, O LORD, [a]at an acceptable time;

O God, in the [b]greatness of Your loving-kindness,

Answer me with [1]Your saving truth.

14 Deliver me from the [a]mire and do not let me sink;

May I be [b]delivered from [1]my foes and from the [2a]deep waters.

15 May the [1a]flood of water not overflow me

Nor the deep swallow me up,

Nor the [b]pit shut its mouth on me.

Psa. 69:16 Answer me, O LORD, for [a]Your loving-kindness is good;

[b]According to the greatness of Your compassion, [c]turn to me,

אֲכָלַתְנִי וְחֶרְפּוֹת חוֹרְפֶיךָ
נָפְלוּ עָלָי ׃ 11 וָאֶבְכֶּה בַצּוֹם
נַפְשִׁי וַתְּהִי לַחֲרָפוֹת לִי ׃ 12
וָאֶתְּנָה לְבוּשִׁי שָׂק וָאֱהִי
לָהֶם לְמָשָׁל ׃ 13 יָשִׂיחוּ בִי
יֹשְׁבֵי שָׁעַר וּנְגִינוֹת שׁוֹתֵי
שֵׁכָר ׃ 14 וַאֲנִי תְפִלָּתִי־לְךָ |
יְהוָה עֵת רָצוֹן אֱלֹהִים בְּרָב־
חַסְדֶּךָ עֲנֵנִי בֶּאֱמֶת יִשְׁעֶךָ ׃ 15
הַצִּילֵנִי מִטִּיט וְאַל־אֶטְבָּעָה
אִנָּצְלָה מִשֹּׂנְאַי וּמִמַּעֲמַקֵּי־
מָיִם ׃ 16 אַל־תִּשְׁטְפֵנִי |
שִׁבֹּלֶת מַיִם וְאַל־תִּבְלָעֵנִי
מְצוּלָה וְאַל־תֶּאְטַר־עָלַי
בְּאֵר פִּיהָ ׃ 17 עֲנֵנִי יְהוָה כִּי־
טוֹב חַסְדֶּךָ כְּרֹב רַחֲמֶיךָ
פְּנֵה אֵלָי ׃ 18 וְאַל־תַּסְתֵּר
פָּנֶיךָ מֵעַבְדֶּךָ כִּי־צַר־לִי
מַהֵר עֲנֵנִי ׃ 19 קָרְבָה אֶל־
נַפְשִׁי גְאָלָהּ לְמַעַן אֹיְבַי
פְּדֵנִי ׃ 20 אַתָּה יָדַעְתָּ חֶרְפָּתִי
וּבָשְׁתִּי וּכְלִמָּתִי נֶגְדְּךָ כָּל־
צוֹרְרָי ׃ 21 חֶרְפָּה | שָׁבְרָה

17 And *[a]*do not hide Your face from Your servant,

For I am *[b]*in distress; answer me quickly.

18 Oh draw near to my soul *and* *[a]*redeem it;

*[b]*Ransom me because of my enemies!

19 You know my *[a]*reproach and my shame and my dishonor;

All my adversaries are [1]before You.

Psa. 69:20 Reproach has *[a]*broken my heart and I am so sick.

And *[b]*I looked for sympathy, but there was none,

And for *[c]*comforters, but I found none.

21 They also gave me [1]*[a]*gall [2]for my food

And for my thirst they *[b]*gave me vinegar to drink.

Psa. 69:22 May *[a]*their table before them become a snare;

And [1]*[b]*when they are in peace, *may it become* a trap.

23 May their *[a]*eyes grow dim so that they cannot see,

And make their *[b]*loins shake continually.

24 *[a]*Pour out Your indignation on them,

And may Your burning anger overtake them.

25 May their [1]*[a]*camp be desolate;

May none dwell in their tents.

26 For they have *[a]*persecuted him whom *[b]*You Yourself have smitten,

לִבִּי וָאָנוּשָׁה וָאֲקַוֶּה לָנוּד
וָאַיִן וְלַמְנַחֲמִים וְלֹא
מָצָאתִי ׃ 22 וַיִּתְּנוּ בְּבָרוּתִי
רֹאשׁ וְלִצְמָאִי יַשְׁקוּנִי חֹמֶץ ׃
23 יְהִי־שֻׁלְחָנָם לִפְנֵיהֶם לְפָח
וְלִשְׁלוֹמִים לְמוֹקֵשׁ ׃ 24
תֶּחְשַׁכְנָה עֵינֵיהֶם מֵרְאוֹת
וּמָתְנֵיהֶם תָּמִיד הַמְעַד ׃ 25
שְׁפָךְ־עֲלֵיהֶם זַעְמֶךָ וַחֲרוֹן
אַפְּךָ יַשִּׂיגֵם ׃ 26 תְּהִי־טִירָתָם
נְשַׁמָּה בְּאָהֳלֵיהֶם אַל־יְהִי
יֹשֵׁב ׃ 27 כִּי־אַתָּה אֲשֶׁר־
הִכִּיתָ רָדָפוּ וְאֶל־מַכְאוֹב
חֲלָלֶיךָ יְסַפֵּרוּ ׃ 28 תְּנָה־עָוֹן
עַל־עֲוֹנָם וְאַל־יָבֹאוּ
בְּצִדְקָתֶךָ ׃ 29 יִמָּחוּ מִסֵּפֶר
חַיִּים וְעִם צַדִּיקִים אַל־
יִכָּתֵבוּ ׃ 30 וַאֲנִי עָנִי וְכוֹאֵב
יְשׁוּעָתְךָ אֱלֹהִים תְּשַׂגְּבֵנִי ׃ 31
אֲהַלְלָה שֵׁם־אֱלֹהִים בְּשִׁיר
וַאֲגַדְּלֶנּוּ בְתוֹדָה ׃ 32 וְתִיטַב
לַיהוָה מִשּׁוֹר פָּר מַקְרִן
מַפְרִיס ׃ 33 רָאוּ עֲנָוִים

And they tell of the pain of those whom [c]You have [1]wounded.
27 Add [a]iniquity to their iniquity,
And [b]may they not come into [c]Your righteousness.
28 May they be [a]blotted out of the [b]book of life
And may they not be [1c]recorded with the righteous.

Psa. 69:29 But I am [a]afflicted and in pain;
[1]May Your salvation, O God, [b]set me *securely* on high.
30 I will [a]praise the name of God with song
And [b]magnify Him with [c]thanksgiving.
31 And it will [a]please the LORD better than an ox
Or a young bull with horns and hoofs.
32 The [a]humble [1]have seen *it and* are glad;
You who seek God, [b]let your heart [2]revive.
33 For [a]the LORD hears the needy
And [b]does not despise His *who are* prisoners.

Psa. 69:34 Let [a]heaven and earth praise Him,
The seas and [b]everything that moves in them.
35 For God will [a]save Zion and [b]build the cities of Judah,
That they may dwell there and [c]possess it.
36 The [1a]descendants of His servants will inherit it,

יִשְׂמְח֖וּ דֹּרְשֵׁ֥י אֱלֹהִֽים וִיחִ֖י
לְבַבְכֶֽם ׃ 34 כִּי־שֹׁמֵ֣עַ אֶל־
אֶבְיוֹנִ֥ים יְהוָ֑ה וְאֶת־אֲסִירָ֗יו
לֹ֣א בָזָֽה ׃ 35 יְֽהַלְל֗וּהוּ שָׁמַ֥יִם
וָאָ֑רֶץ יַ֝מִּ֗ים וְכָל־רֹמֵ֥שׂ בָּֽם ׃
36 כִּ֤י אֱלֹהִ֨ים ׀ יוֹשִׁ֬יעַ צִיּ֗וֹן
וְ֭יִבְנֶה עָרֵ֣י יְהוּדָ֑ה וְיָ֥שְׁב֥וּ שָׁ֗ם
וִֽירֵשֽׁוּהָ ׃ 37 וְזֶ֣רַע עֲבָדָ֣יו
יִנְחָל֑וּהָ וְאֹהֲבֵ֥י שְׁמ֗וֹ יִשְׁכְּנוּ־
בָֽהּ ׃

And those who love His name [b]will dwell in it.	

References

Psalm 69:0
†Or possibly *Lilies*

Psalm 69:1
¹Lit *come to the soul*
*a*Job 22:11; Ps 32:6; 42:7; 69:14, 15; Jon 2:5

Psalm 69:2
¹Lit *flowing stream*
*a*Ps 40:2
*b*Jon 2:3

Psalm 69:3
*a*Ps 6:6
*b*Deut 28:32; Ps 38:10; 119:82, 123; Is 38:14

Psalm 69:4
¹Or *silence*
*a*Ps 35:19; John 15:25
*b*Ps 35:19; 38:19; 59:3
*c*Ps 35:11; Jer 15:10

Psalm 69:5
*a*Ps 38:5
*b*Ps 44:21

Psalm 69:6
¹Heb *YHWH,* usually rendered *LORD*
*a*2 Sam 12:14

Psalm 69:7
*a*Jer 15:15
*b*Ps 44:15; Is 50:6; Jer 51:51

Psalm 69:8
¹Lit *to*
*a*Job 19:13-15; Ps 31:11; 38:11

Psalm 69:9
[a]Ps 119:139; John 2:17
[b]Ps 89:41, 50; Rom 15:3

Psalm 69:10
[a]Ps 35:13

Psalm 69:11
[a]1 Kin 20:31; Ps 35:13
[b]1 Kin 9:7; Job 17:6; Ps 44:14; Jer 24:9

Psalm 69:12
[1]Lit *songs*
[a]Gen 19:1; Ruth 4:1
[b]Job 30:9

Psalm 69:13
[1]Or *the faithfulness of Your salvation*
[a]Ps 32:6; Is 49:8; 2 Cor 6:2
[b]Ps 51:1

Psalm 69:14
[1]Lit *those who hate me*
[2]Lit *deep places of water*
[a]Ps 69:2
[b]Ps 144:7

Psalm 69:15
[1]Lit *stream*
[a]Ps 124:4, 5
[b]Num 16:33; Ps 28:1; 141:7

Psalm 69:16
[a]Ps 63:3; 109:21
[b]Ps 51:1; 106:45
[c]Ps 25:16; 86:16

Psalm 69:17
[a]Ps 27:9; 102:2; 143:7
[b]Ps 31:9; 66:14

Psalm 69:18
[a]2 Sam 4:9; Ps 26:11; 49:15
[b]Ps 119:134

Psalm 69:19
[1]Or known *to You*
[a]Ps 22:6; 31:11

Psalm 69:20
[a]Jer 23:9
[b]Ps 142:4; Is 63:5
Job 16:2

Psalm 69:21
[1]Or *poison*
[2]Or *in*
[a]Deut 29:18
[b]Matt 27:34, 48; Mark 15:23, 36; Luke 23:36; John 19:28-30

Psalm 69:22
[1]Lit *for those who are secure*
[a]Rom 11:9, 10
[b]1 Thess 5:3

Psalm 69:23
[a]Is 6:10
[b]Dan 5:6

Psalm 69:24
[a]Ps 79:6; Jer 10:25; Ezek 20:8; Hos 5:10

Psalm 69:25
[1]Lit *encampment*
[a]Matt 23:38; Luke 13:35; Acts 1:20

Psalm 69:26
[1]Lit *pierced*
[a]2 Chr 28:9; Zech 1:15
[b]Is 53:4
[c]Ps 109:22

Psalm 69:27
[a]Neh 4:5; Ps 109:14; Rom 1:28
[b]Is 26:10
[c]Ps 103:17

Psalm 69:28
[1]Lit *written*
[a]Ex 32:32, 33; Rev 3:5
[b]Phil 4:3; Rev 13:8; 17:8; 20:15
[c]Ps 87:6; Ezek 13:9; Luke 10:20; Heb 12:23

Psalm 69:29
[1]Or *Your salvation, O God, will set...*
[a]Ps 70:5
[b]Ps 20:1; 59:1

Psalm 69:30
[a]Ps 28:7
[b]Ps 34:3
[c]Ps 50:14

Psalm 69:31
[a]Ps 50:13, 14; 51:16

Psalm 69:32
[1]Some mss and ancient versions read *will see*
[2]Or *live*
[a]Ps 34:2
[b]Ps 22:26

Psalm 69:33
[a]Ps 12:5
[b]Ps 68:6

Psalm 69:34
[a]Ps 96:11; 98:7; 148:1-13; Is 44:23; 49:13
[b]Is 55:12

Psalm 69:35
[a]Ps 46:5; 51:18
[b]Ps 147:2; Is 44:26

[c]Obad 17

Psalm 69:36
[1]Lit *seed*
[a]Ps 25:13; 102:28
[b]Ps 37:29

Targum

Psa. 69:1 For praise; concerning the exiles of the Sanhedrin; composed by David. ² Redeem me, O God, for an army of sinners has come to trouble me, like water that has reached to the soul. ³ I am sunk in exile like water of the deep, and there is no place to stand; I have come to the mighty depths; a band of wicked men and a wicked king have sent me into exile. ⁴ I am weary of calling out, my throat has become rough, my eyes have ceased to wait for my God. ⁵ Those who hate me without a cause are more numerous that the hairs of my head; those who dismay me – my enemies, false witnesses – have grown strong; what I never stole I will [have to] repay, because of their false witness. ⁶ O God, you know my folly; my sins have not been hidden from your presence. ⁷ Those who trust in you will not be disappointed in me; those who seek instruction from you will not be ashamed of me, O God of Israel. ⁸ For on your account I have borne disgrace; shame has covered my face. ⁹ I have been accounted a stranger to my brothers, and [I am] like a Gentile to the sons of my mother. ¹⁰ For zeal for the sanctuary has consumed me; and the condemnation of the wicked who condemn you when they prefer their idols to your glory has fallen on me. ¹¹ And I wept in the fasting of my soul; and my kindness became my shame. ¹² And I put sackcloth in place of my clothing; and I became a proverb to them. ¹³ Those who sit in the gate will speak about me in the marketplace, and [in] the songs of those who come to drink liquor in the circuses. ¹⁴ But as for me, my prayer is in your presence, O LORD, in the time of favor; O God, in the abundance of your goodness answer me in the truth of your redemption. ¹⁵ Deliver me from exile, which is likened to mud, and I will not sink; let me be delivered from my enemies, who are like the depths of waters. ¹⁶ A mighty king will not send me into exile, and the powerful deep will not swallow me to cover me up, and the mouth of Gehenna will not be opened up for me. ¹⁷ Answer me, O LORD, for your kindness is good; look towards me with the abundance of your compassion. ¹⁸ And do not remove your presence from your servant, for I am in distress; hasten, answer me. ¹⁹ Draw near to my soul, redeem it, so that my enemies may not claim superiority over me, redeem me. ²⁰ You know my disgrace and my shame and my dishonor; before you stand all my oppressors. ²¹ Disgrace has broken my heart, and behold, it is ill; and I waited for those skilled in mourning, but they were not; and for those skilled in comfort, and I found them not. ²² And as my meal they gave me bitter gall and poison; and for my thirst, they gave me vinegar to drink. ²³ Let their table that they set before me with my food become a snare before them; and their sacrifices an offense. ²⁴ Let their eyes darken so they cannot see, and let their loins continually tremble. ²⁵ Pour out your anger upon them, and may your harsh anger overtake them. ²⁶ Let their tent became deserted, may no one settle in their tent. ²⁷ For they have pursued the one you have smitten, and they shall tell of the one wounded for your slain. ²⁸ Give iniquity for their iniquity, and let them not be purified to enter the assembly of your righteous ones. ²⁹ Let them be erased from the memorial book of life, and let them not be written with the righteous. [30] But I am poor and wounded; your redemption, O God, will save me. [31] I will praise the name of my God with song, and I will magnify him with thanksgiving. [32] And my prayer will be more pleasing in the presence of the LORD than a choice fatted ox that the first Adam sacrificed, whose horns preceded its hooves. [33] The humble have seen; so let those who seek instruction from the presence of God be glad and let their heart live. [34] For the LORD accepts the prayer of the lowly, and has not despised his prisoners. [35] Let the angels of heaven and those who dwell on earth praise him; the seas, and all that swarms in them. [36] For God will redeem Zion and repair the cities of Judah, and they will return thither and inherit it. [37] And the sons of his servants will succeed to it, and those who love his name will abide in its midst.

Spiritual Awareness

Due to the length of the Psalm, only the spiritual awareness of verses will be explored.

Introduction

Jewish history is that even though the people were exiled from their homeland, thus living on foreign soil for centuries, the nation grew and prospered. In 1948 the nation of Israel was reestablished on the land that the LORD promised to give Abraham and his descendants.

A rose is delicate and protected by the thorns that surround it. This is a metaphor for Israel. She is delicate and is protected by the Torah, which surrounds her. This Psalm is a prophetic vision of David that generations of brave Jews survived the dark centuries of exile.

Superscript

The Psalmist reminds Israel that she is in danger of attack and that only the LORD can protect her.

To the Sefirah Netzach who offers victory, upon roses, by David.

Verse one

David is saying that a whirlpool plunging into the deep had grabbed him and was taking him down. He was in dire need of the LORD to save his soul. The depths would have taken him to Sheol.

Help me, O God, for the waters have penetrated unto my soul.

Verse four

Israel did not find sympathy from the nations of the world. The nations that housed hostile feelings against her were ready to destroy her. The Psalmist requested the ability to restore Israel after her enemies ruined her.

They that hate me without reason are more than the hairs of my head; mighty are they that would make me numb, that unjustly come forward as my foes so that I might restore that which I have never taken away.

Verse eight

David was speaking for Israel. It is acknowledged that the other nations of the world are also the children of the LORD because the LORD is the Father of all humanity, and therefore, they should have recognized Israel as a sister nation.

I became to my brothers as a man unworthy of rights and an alien to the sons of my mother.

Verse thirteen

David calls out to the Sefirah Chesed for the LORD's loving-kindness.

But as for me, my prayer shall be to You, O God, for one instant of favor; O God, who even while judging remains in the abundance of loving kindness from the Sefirah Chesed, answer me with the truth of Your salvation.

Verse eighteen

The redemption of Israel by the LORD teaches the nations of the world that they, too, need to examine their morals and ethics so that the godless humans will not ruin them.

Draw nearer to my soul, and redeem it; ransom me because of my enemies.

Verse twenty-three

With the sensual depravity of the nations, they will lose the clarity of spiritual perception.

That their eyes may become darkened so that they cannot see and let their loins tremble continually.

Verse thirty

The nations that conquered Israel thought that the LORD had abandoned them. When the Babylonians invaded Judah, it was not much of a fight. They believed that the LORD had abandoned Israel. However, Israel never lost faith in the LORD.

But as far for me, afflicted and in pain, Your salvation, O God, shall set me up on high.

112

Psalm 70

New American Standard 1995	Hebrew

Psa. 70:0 For the choir director. *A Psalm* of David; for a memorial.
 	
Psa. 70:1 [a]O God, *hasten* to deliver me;
  O LORD, hasten to my help!
2 [a]Let those be ashamed and humiliated
  Who seek my [1]life;
  Let those be turned back and dishonored
  Who delight [2]in my hurt.
3 [a]Let those be [1]turned back because of their shame
  Who say, "Aha, aha!"
 	
Psa. 70:4 Let all who seek You rejoice and be glad in You;
  And let those who love Your salvation say continually,
  "Let God be magnified."
5 But [a]I am afflicted and needy;
  [b]Hasten to me, O God!
  You are my help and my deliverer;
  O LORD, do not delay.
	Psa. 70:1 לַמְנַצֵּחַ לְדָוִד
	לְהַזְכִּיר׃ 2 אֱלֹהִים לְהַצִּילֵנִי
	יְהוָה לְעֶזְרָתִי חוּשָׁה׃ 3 יֵבֹשׁוּ
	וְיַחְפְּרוּ מְבַקְשֵׁי נַפְשִׁי יִסֹּגוּ
	אָחוֹר וְיִכָּלְמוּ חֲפֵצֵי רָעָתִי׃
	4 יָשׁוּבוּ עַל־עֵקֶב בָּשְׁתָּם
	הָאֹמְרִים הֶאָח ׀ הֶאָח׃ 5
	יָשִׂישׂוּ וְיִשְׂמְחוּ ׀ בְּךָ כָּל־
	מְבַקְשֶׁיךָ וְיֹאמְרוּ תָמִיד
	יִגְדַּל אֱלֹהִים אֹהֲבֵי
	יְשׁוּעָתֶךָ׃ 6 וַאֲנִי ׀ עָנִי
	וְאֶבְיוֹן אֱלֹהִים חוּשָׁה־לִּי
	עֶזְרִי וּמְפַלְטִי אַתָּה יְהוָה
	אַל־תְּאַחַר׃

References

Psalm 70:1
[a]Ps 40:13-17; 70:1-5

Psalm 70:2
[1]Or *soul*
[2]Or *to injure me*
[a]Ps 35:4, 26

Psalm 70:3
[1]Some mss read *appalled*
[a]Ps 40:15

Psalm 70:5
[a]Ps 40:17
[b]Ps 141:1

Targum

Psa. 70:1 For praise; composed by David, for remembrance; concerning the handful of incense. [2] O God, [hasten] to deliver us, O LORD, hasten to our aid. [3] Let those who seek my soul be ashamed and disgraced; let those who desire my ruin draw back and be dishonored. [4] Let them turn back, because they lay in wait for me; let those who say about me "We have rejoiced, rejoiced!" be punished as befits their shame. [5] Let those who seek instruction from you be glad and exult in your word, and let those who love your redemption always say, "May the glory of the LORD be magnified." [6] But I am poor and lowly, O God; hasten to me, you are my help and salvation; O LORD, do not delay.

Spiritual Awareness

Introduction

In this Psalm, David pleaded for his return to power. The following parable fits the situation.

A king became vexed at the shepherd. He chased away the flock, tore down the animal shed, and dismissed the shepherd. After a time, the king gathered the sheep and rebuilt the shed. The king did not restore the shepherd to his position. The shepherd lamented, "Behold the sheep are gathered in, the shed is rebuilt, but I am not remembered.

Superscript

To the Sefirah Netzach who grants victory. By David, to serve as a memorial.

Verse one

David makes a twofold appeal to the LORD. The first appeal is for a judgment that would frustrate the criminal intentions of his foes. The second is to deliver him from their hands.

O God, make hast to deliver me, to help me, O God.

Verse two

Only by failing can ordinary people become aware that they have been evil in the past and are still morally unworthy.

So that they may be deceived and unmasked, those that seek my soul; that they may fall back and be ashamed, those who desire my hurt.

Verse three

Only by humiliation can evil people be made to return to the LORD.

Let them turn back by reason of their shame, those who would call out even now: O brother, brother!

Verse four

David believed that if the LORD delivered him back into power that his enemies would realize the evil that they were doing.

But let all those that seek You blossom forth blissfully and rejoice in You, and let such as love your salvation say at all times: God reveals his greatness.

Verse five

But I am poor and defenseless, O God, make haste unto me. You are my help and my deliverer; O God, do not tarry.

Complete Psalm Rewrite Emphasizing Spiritual Awareness

To the Sefirah Netzach who grants victory. By David, to serve as a memorial.

O God, make hast to deliver me, to help me, O God.

So that they may be deceived and unmasked, those that seek my soul; that they may fall back and be ashamed, those who desire my hurt.

Let them turn back by reason of their shame, those who would call out even now: O brother, brother!

But let all those that seek You blossom forth blissfully and rejoice in You, and let such as love your salvation say at all times: God reveals his greatness.

But I am poor and defenseless, O God, make haste unto me. You are my help and my deliverer; O God, do not tarry.

APPENDIX

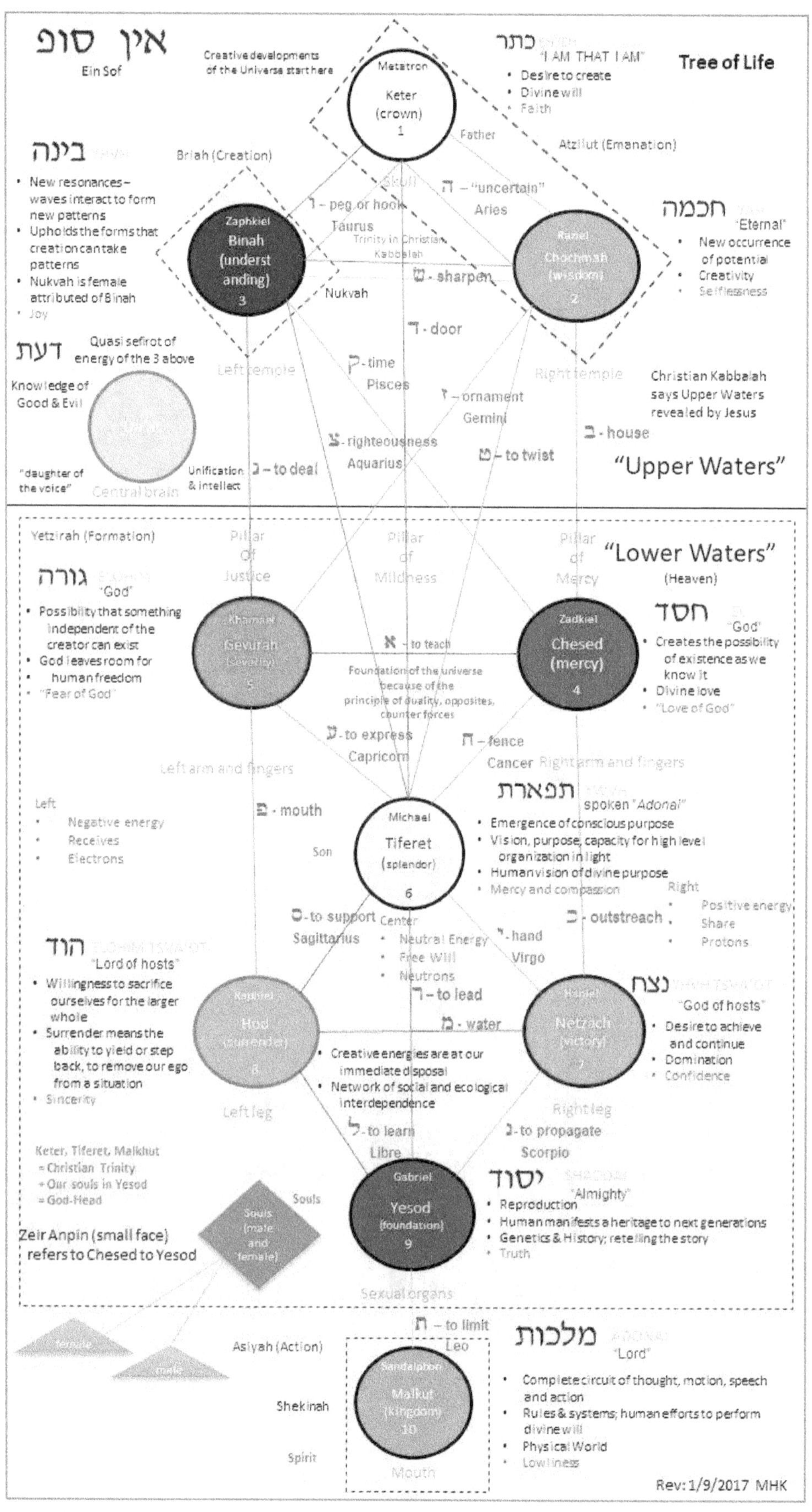

אין סוף
Ein Sof
Tree of Life
כתר
"I AM THAT I AM"
• Desire to create
• Divine will
• Faith
Creative developments of the Universe start here
Metatron
Keter (crown) 1
Father
Briah (Creation)
Atzilut (Emanation)
בינה
• New resonances – waves interact to form new patterns
• Upholds the forms that creation can take patterns
• Nukvah is female attributed of Binah
• Joy
Zaphkiel
Binah (understanding) 3
ו – peg or hook
Taurus
Trinity in Christian Kabbalah
Nukvah
ה – "uncertain"
Aries
חכמה
"Eternal"
• New occurrence of potential
• Creativity
• Selflessness
Raziel
Chochmah (wisdom) 2
ש - sharpen
ד - door
דעת
Quasi sefirot of energy of the 3 above
Knowledge of Good & Evil
ק - time
Pisces
ז – ornament
Gemini
"daughter of the voice"
ב - house
Christian Kabbalah says Upper Waters revealed by Jesus
Left temple
Right temple
צ - righteousness
Aquarius
ט – to twist
Unification & intellect
נ – to deal
"Upper Waters"
Central brain
Yetzirah (Formation)
"Lower Waters"
(Heaven)
Pillar Of Justice
Pillar of Mildness
Pillar of Mercy
גורה
"God"
• Possibility that something independent of the creator can exist
• God leaves room for human freedom
• "Fear of God"
Khamael
Gevurah (severity) 5
א – to teach
Foundation of the universe because of the principle of duality, opposites, counter forces
חסד
"God"
• Creates the possibility of existence as we know it
• Divine love
• "Love of God"
Zadkiel
Chesed (mercy) 4
ע - to express
Capricorn
ח – fence
Cancer
Left arm and fingers
Right arm and fingers
Left
• Negative energy
• Receives
• Electrons
פ - mouth
תפארת
spoken "Adonai"
• Emergence of conscious purpose
• Vision, purpose, capacity for high level organization in light
• Human vision of divine purpose
• Mercy and compassion
Michael
Tiferet (splendor) 6
Son
Center
• Neutral Energy
• Free Will
• Neutrons
ר - outstreach
Right
• Positive energy
• Share
• Protons
ס - to support
Sagittarius
י - hand
Virgo
ר – to lead
הוד
"Lord of hosts"
• Willingness to sacrifice ourselves for the larger whole
• Surrender means the ability to yield or step back, to remove our ego from a situation
• Sincerity
Raphael
Hod (surrender) 8
מ - water
Creative energies are at our immediate disposal
Network of social and ecological interdependence
נצח
"God of hosts"
• Desire to achieve and continue
• Domination
• Confidence
Haniel
Netzach (victory) 7
Left leg
Right leg
Keter, Tiferet, Malkhut
= Christian Trinity
+ Our souls in Yesod
= God-Head
ל - to learn
Libre
נ - to propagate
Scorpio
יסוד
"Almighty"
• Reproduction
• Human manifests a heritage to next generations
• Genetics & History; retelling the story
• Truth
Gabriel
Yesod (foundation) 9
Zeir Anpin (small face) refers to Chesed to Yesod
Souls
Souls (male and female)
Sexual organs
ת – to limit
Leo
מלכות
"Lord"
• Complete circuit of thought, motion, speech and action
• Rules & systems; human efforts to perform divine will
• Physical World
• Lowliness
Asiyah (Action)
Female
male
Sandalphon
Malkut (kingdom) 10
Shekinah
Spirit
Mouth
Rev: 1/9/2017 MHK

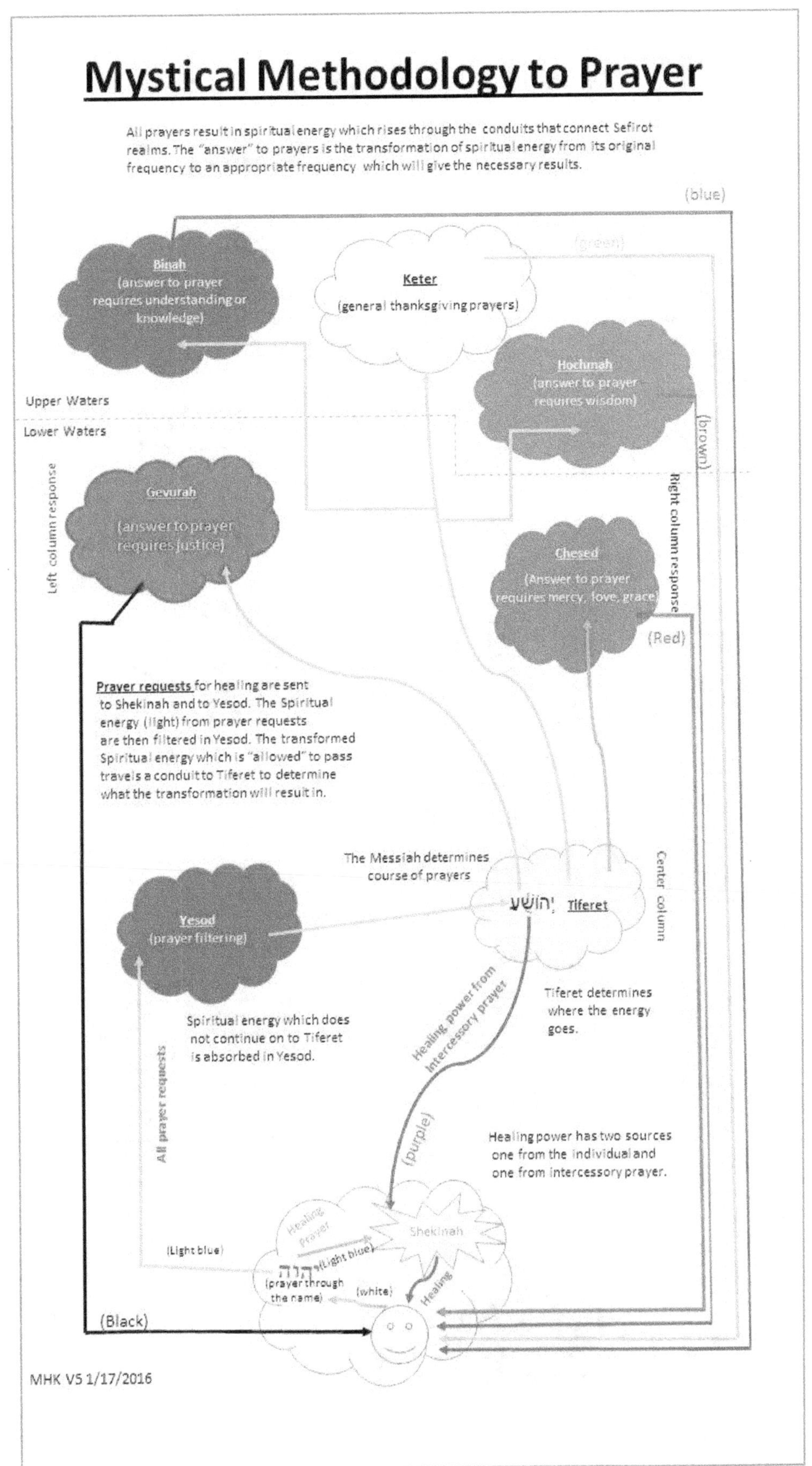

Mystical Methodology to Prayer
All prayers result in spiritual energy which rises through the conduits that connect Sefirot realms. The "answer" to prayers is the transformation of spiritual energy from its original frequency to an appropriate frequency which will give the necessary results.
(blue)
(green)
Binah
(answer to prayer requires understanding or knowledge)
Keter
(general thanksgiving prayers)
Hochmah
(answer to prayer requires wisdom)
Upper Waters
Lower Waters
(brown)
Left column response
Gevurah
(answer to prayer requires justice)
Chesed
(Answer to prayer requires mercy, love, grace)
Right column response
(Red)
Prayer requests for healing are sent to Shekinah and to Yesod. The Spiritual energy (light) from prayer requests are then filtered in Yesod. The transformed Spiritual energy which is "allowed" to pass travels a conduit to Tiferet to determine what the transformation will result in.
The Messiah determines course of prayers
יהושע Tiferet
Center column
Yesod
(prayer filtering)
Tiferet determines where the energy goes.
Healing power from intercessory prayer
Spiritual energy which does not continue on to Tiferet is absorbed in Yesod.
All prayer requests
(purple)
Healing power has two sources one from the individual and one from intercessory prayer.
Healing Prayer
Shekinah
(Light blue)
(light blue)
יהוה
(prayer through the name)
(white)
Healing
(Black)
MHK V5 1/17/2016

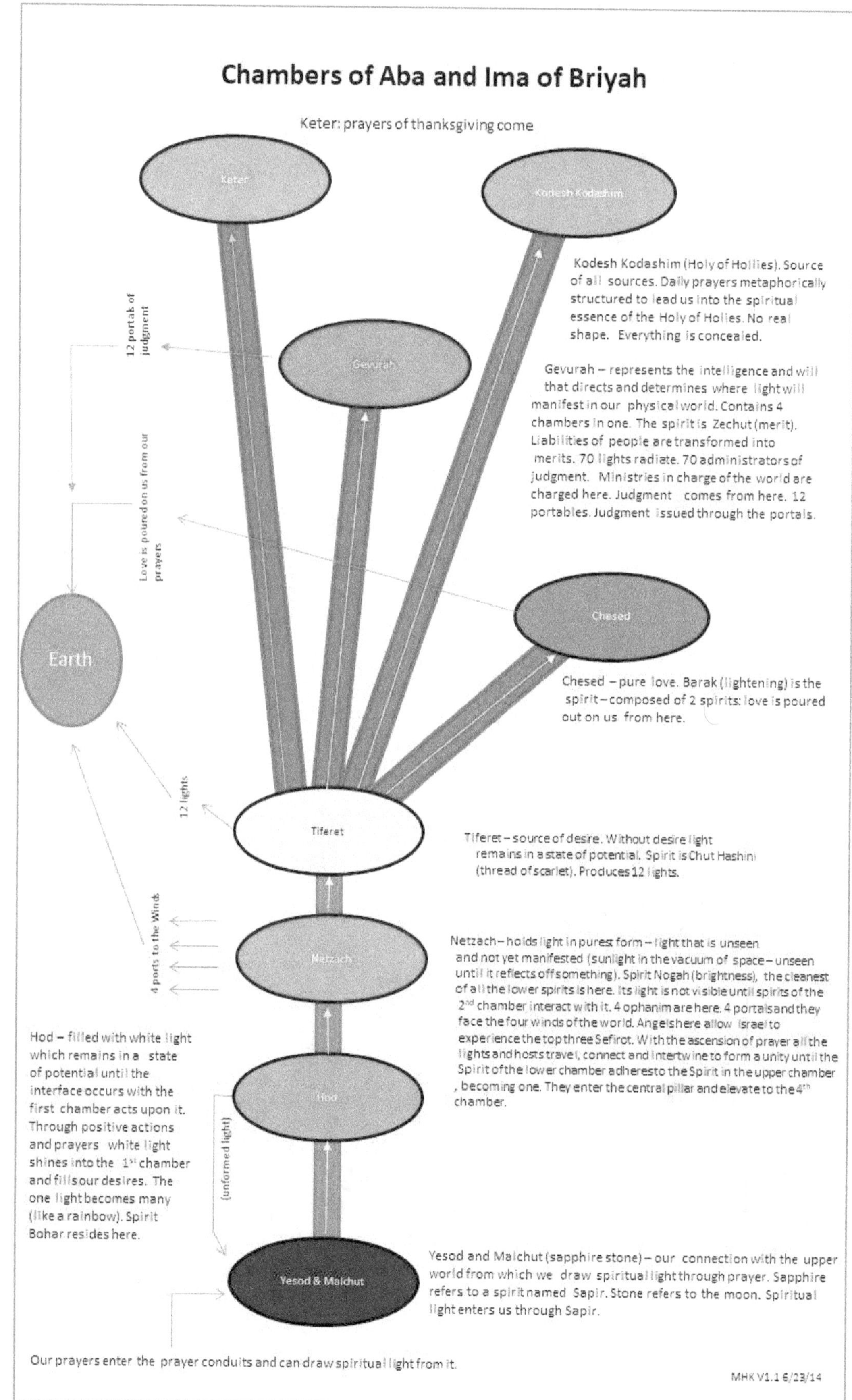

Chambers of Aba and Ima of Briyah
Keter: prayers of thanksgiving come
Keter
Kodesh Kodashim
Gevurah
Chesed
Earth
Tiferet
Netzach
Hod
Yesod & Malchut
12 portals of judgment
Love is poured on us from our prayers
12 lights
4 ports to the Winds
(unformed light)
Kodesh Kodashim (Holy of Hollies). Source of all sources. Daily prayers metaphorically structured to lead us into the spiritual essence of the Holy of Hollies. No real shape. Everything is concealed.
Gevurah – represents the intelligence and will that directs and determines where light will manifest in our physical world. Contains 4 chambers in one. The spirit is Zechut (merit). Liabilities of people are transformed into merits. 70 lights radiate. 70 administrators of judgment. Ministries in charge of the world are charged here. Judgment comes from here. 12 portables. Judgment issued through the portals.
Chesed – pure love. Barak (lightening) is the spirit – composed of 2 spirits: love is poured out on us from here.
Tiferet – source of desire. Without desire light remains in a state of potential. Spirit is Chut Hashini (thread of scarlet). Produces 12 lights.
Netzach – holds light in purest form – light that is unseen and not yet manifested (sunlight in the vacuum of space – unseen until it reflects off something). Spirit Nogah (brightness), the cleanest of all the lower spirits is here. Its light is not visible until spirits of the 2nd chamber interact with it. 4 ophanim are here. 4 portals and they face the four winds of the world. Angels here allow Israel to experience the top three Sefirot. With the ascension of prayer all the lights and hosts travel, connect and intertwine to form a unity until the Spirit of the lower chamber adheres to the Spirit in the upper chamber, becoming one. They enter the central pillar and elevate to the 4th chamber.
Hod – filled with white light which remains in a state of potential until the interface occurs with the first chamber acts upon it. Through positive actions and prayers white light shines into the 1st chamber and fills our desires. The one light becomes many (like a rainbow). Spirit Bohar resides here.
Yesod and Malchut (sapphire stone) – our connection with the upper world from which we draw spiritual light through prayer. Sapphire refers to a spirit named Sapir. Stone refers to the moon. Spiritual light enters us through Sapir.
Our prayers enter the prayer conduits and can draw spiritual light from it.
MHK V1.1 6/23/14

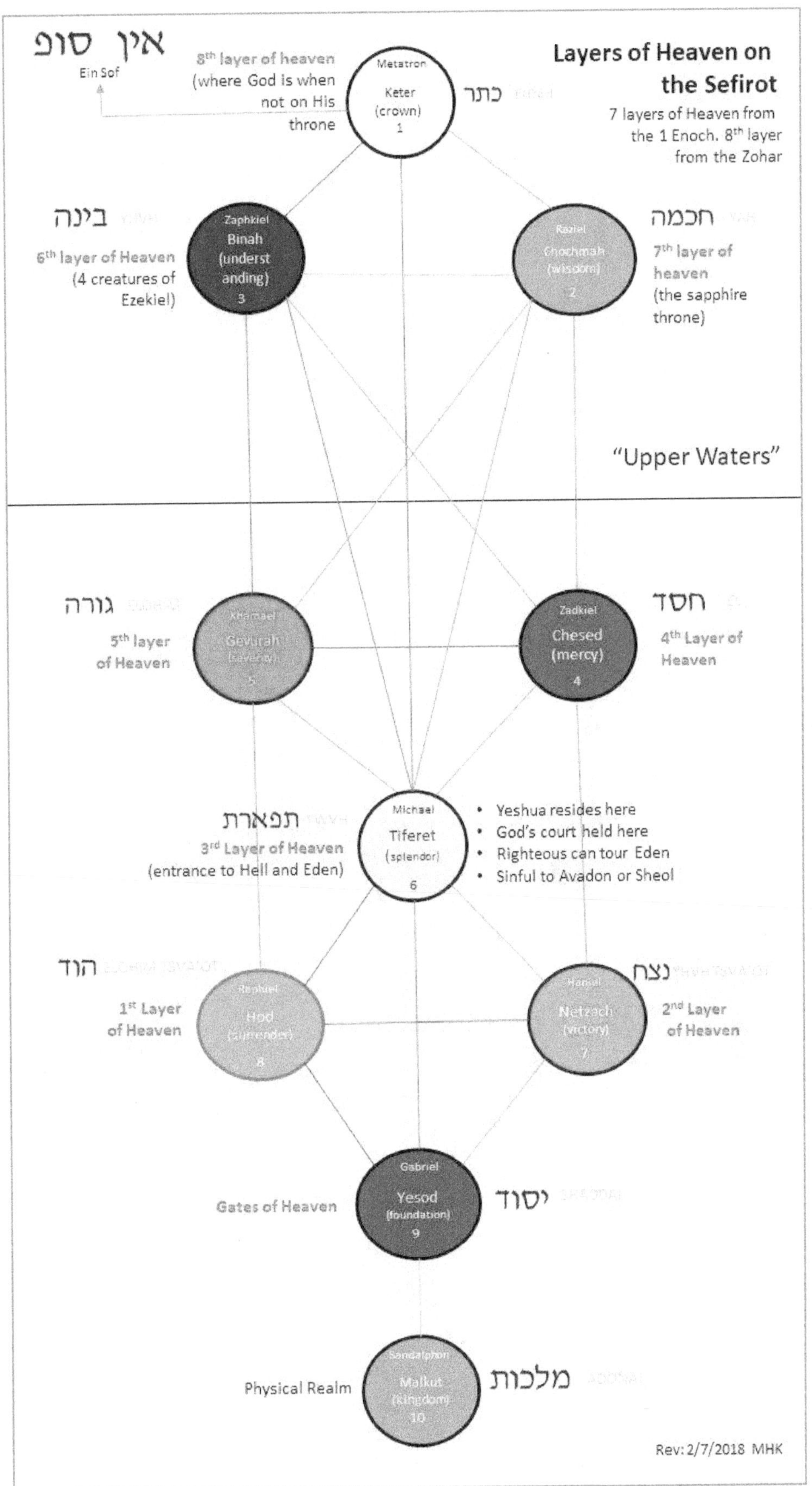
אין סוף
Ein Sof

8th layer of heaven (where God is when not on His throne)

Layers of Heaven on the Sefirot
7 layers of Heaven from the 1 Enoch. 8th layer from the Zohar

Metatron
Keter
(crown)
1

כתר

בינה
6th layer of Heaven (4 creatures of Ezekiel)

Zaphkiel
Binah
(understanding)
3

חכמה
7th layer of heaven (the sapphire throne)

Raziel
Chochmah
(wisdom)
2

"Upper Waters"

גורה
5th layer of Heaven

Khamael
Gevurah
(severity)
5

חסד
4th Layer of Heaven

Zadkiel
Chesed
(mercy)
4

תפארת
3rd Layer of Heaven (entrance to Hell and Eden)

Michael
Tiferet
(splendor)
6

• Yeshua resides here
• God's court held here
• Righteous can tour Eden
• Sinful to Avadon or Sheol

הוד
1st Layer of Heaven

Raphael
Hod
(surrender)
8

נצח
2nd Layer of Heaven

Haniel
Netzach
(victory)
7

Gabriel
Yesod
(foundation)
9

יסוד

Gates of Heaven

Sandalphon
Malkut
(kingdom)
10

מלכות

Physical Realm

Rev: 2/7/2018 MHK